DO JEWS, CHRISTIANS, & MUSLIMS WORSHIP THE SAME GOD?

DO JEWS, CHRISTIANS, & MUSLIMS WORSHIP THE SAME GOD?

JACOB
NEUSNER

BARUCH A.
LEVINE

BRUCE D.
CHILTON

VINCENT J.
CORNELL

EPILOGUE BY MARTIN E. MARTY

DO JEWS, CHRISTIANS, AND MUSLIMS WORSHIP THE SAME GOD?

This book is printed on acid-free paper.

Library of Congress Cataloging-in-Publication Data has been requested.

ISBN 978-1-4267-5237-7

Scripture translations are by the individual authors.

Translation of *Justin's Apology* is by Bruce D. Chilton.

12 13 14 15 16 17 18 19 20 21—10 9 8 7 6 5 4 3 2 1

MANUFACTURED IN THE UNITED STATES OF AMERICA

Contents

Preface

Many Jews, Muslims, and Christians are devout, faithful, and law-abiding; yet on any given day, it is not possible to watch current events without seeing vigorous and heated disputes among them, whether over construction of the "ground zero" mosque, lobbying of state legislatures against Sharia law, sharing worship space, fallout of the Arab Spring, or protecting civil rights, the security of Jerusalem, or even the authority of sacred texts. With so much rancor, can there be any common ground? Do we even worship the same God? And can religion, which historically has been so divisive, be any help at all?

These questions, and particularly the question of whether or not Jews, Christians, and Muslims worship the same God, act as the frame within which Jacob Neusner, Baruch Levine, Bruce Chilton, and Vincent Cornell write. Representing Judaism, Christianity, and Islam within the American context, these religious authorities set out to tackle this deceptively simple question. Then in the epilogue Martin Marty, using the previous chapters as guides, boldly states how the conversation can proceed even further.

Baruch Levine and Jacob Neusner represent Judaism; Bruce Chilton represents Christianity, and Vincent Cornell represents Islam. Each recognizes that monotheistic religions resemble one another in maintaining the unity of God; and therefore monotheist religions *ought* to be construed to worship the same God, but (and there is a but)

vii

real and significant differences cannot be overlooked. And depending on the vantage point, the possibility that these religions do not worship the same God must be initially conceded in order to provide integrity to the entire enterprise.

Some other authors argue that while beliefs about God differ, the object of worship is ultimately the same. This book, however, takes a more pragmatic view. With candor, conviction, and civility these authors take a frank look at the question of whether Jews, Christians, and Muslims worship the same God and then model how religious people can serve as a means to move us all forward with common purpose, rather than act as a wedge that only drives us further apart.

So what lies ahead for the children of Abraham? Interfaith dialogue among them is made possible by monotheism, which defines the common ground on the foundations of which debate can take place, *but only* if all three religions recognize each other as essentially monotheistic. Whether or not Jews, Christians, and Muslims worship the same God, we must find the will (politically, socially, and personally) to continue the process of dialogue despite our differences and focus on the worthy goal of peace with justice for all.

One God: The Enduring Biblical Vision

Baruch A. Levine

Question: Do Jews, Christians, and Muslims all worship the same God? Answer: Yes, of course, *but . . .*

We customarily refer to Judaism, Christianity, and Islam as the three monotheist religions. All three are linked to the Hebrew Bible, where monotheism, as we know it, was first expounded. The New Testament draws heavily on and attributes authority to the Hebrew Bible (the Old Testament), which was incorporated fully into the Christian canon. It is surely reasonable, even inescapable to conclude that the God of the Old and New Testaments is to be identified as one and the same divine being, the God of Abraham. In the relationship of Islam to both Judaism and Christianity, the issue of divine identity, though more complex, evokes the same conclusion. The Qur'an, in its own ways, acknowledges the historic priority of both Judaism and Christianity and endorses the revelation of the Torah to the People of the Book, a designation that can refer to Christians as well as Jews. The

Qur'an often speaks of biblical personalities, Patriarchs, kings, prophets, and others, and appropriates the Hebrew biblical narrative in large part. Muslims are "Children of Abraham" and worship the God of Abraham.

It has been said that there is "a sociology of questions," special factors that explain why certain issues come to the fore when they do. As a result of recent efforts at dialogue, undertaken in free and open societies, Jews and Christians, for their part, have made considerable progress in repairing their religious relationship and in resolving issues between them. (The same can be said for the different Christian churches among themselves). This has been accomplished by emphasizing commonality over difference and by affirming the right to freedom of religion.

The same process is just beginning with respect to Islam and significantly during a period of Islamic resurgence and social and political upheaval in many Arab and/or Muslim societies. In limited circles, Jewish-Christian dialogue has been expanded to include the third monotheist religion, Islam, and in some secular circles there is now more interest in what Islam has to say. We are hearing a still, small voice of reconciliation amidst the clamor of contention coming from every side. By raising the age-old question of "divine identity" we are presumably operating on the premise that the present confrontation between Islam and the West can be addressed more effectively by emphasizing the shared belief in one and the same God; that what has changed for the better in the Jewish-Christian relationship can, as a parallel, be replicated in relations with Islam. Surely, that would be a most welcome outcome.

It must be conceded, however, that in large part, history challenges this premise. The histories of the three monotheist religions show they have often been in conflict, with Christians and Muslims variously prevailing over, or being dominated by, each other and with Jews being restricted, at the very least, by both. There is also a crowded history of Christian and Muslim "sectarian" conflicts.

It must be remembered that open dialogue has been productive only when the requisite political, social, and cultural conditions have been obtained in the several societies so as to allow for it, which is often not the case, and when the will to coexist peacefully is strong enough to resist exclusionary pressures. Ontological determinations, in and of themselves, hardly tell the whole story. This is the qualifying *but* in the answer to our question, cautioning us against unwarranted expectations.

Who Holds the Rights to the One, True God?

In the study to follow, I will focus on historic relationships among the three monotheist confessions, (of which two are vast in number and one severely limited in number), rather than on ontology or on theology as such. I do so with the recognition that it is precisely the "oneness" (=unity) of God that forces the issue of exclusivity in the human-divine encounter. In real time, nations and empires, Christian and Muslim, and others, have fought against each other and competed with each other, and have applied restrictive policies to the Jews within their orbits. So, whose side is God on? The mythological warring among gods is over. All power is now concentrated in one divine being. To put it differently: historically, the issue that has informed conflict among the monotheist religions has been that of rival claims to an exclusive relationship with the one, true God, not that of identifying the universal deity, on which there has generally been theological agreement.

This analysis is borne out by the histories of the three religions. First, there were the Israelites/Jews, who represented themselves as the exclusive recipients of God's revealed word through Moses and the prophets and who considered themselves bound to God by a unique covenant. In the light of events yet to come, the historic priority of the Israelite revelation, recorded in the Hebrew Bible, lends to post-biblical Judaism, the religion of a very small people, a disproportionate degree of importance in the history of religions. Then, there were the Christians, who announced a subsequent revelation that has them

3

assuming the role formerly assigned to the Jewish People. Christianity reconfigured the human-divine encounter by its introduction of a savior, Jesus Christ, son of God. The earlier Israelite revelation is not denied; it remains true as far as it goes, but it is now deemed insufficient—some would say that it had been superseded. Henceforth, the path to God was to be exclusively through Christ, mediator of the New Covenant.

Then, centuries later in Arabia (precisely, in the early seventh century C.E.), revelations from God were transmitted by the Prophet, Muhammad, as preserved in the Qur'an and recorded in Hadith literature. Once again, the preexisting revelations, now of both Old and New Testaments, are acknowledged but are deemed insufficient, or thought to have been superseded. Henceforth, only Islam pronounces God's will and his truth in full. So, we have three religious communities aware that they are worshiping the same God and cognizant of their formative intersections, yet in competition with each other, if not in actual conflict. At certain times in the past, elements within these communities have engaged in dialogue across religious lines, but it has usually been polemical in character. There is also a history of mutual influences. There appears to be no intellectual barrier to communication when there is a desire to communicate; the three groups understand where they are coming from. This is, in briefest outline, the historic background of our problem.

The Dynamic of Competing Monotheisms

The first step in probing the history of competing monotheisms is to recognize that the first Christians were themselves Jews living in the biblical homeland. Initially, they bore a message of redemption to their own people, conveyed through Christ, the Savior, whose Jewish lineage is clearly registered. Very soon, and following in the footsteps of Jewish missionaries, early Christians embarked on missionary activity directed increasingly at the Gentiles of the Roman Empire, but with a critical difference: whereas the early Christians affirmed their commitment to

4

the single God of the Hebrew Bible and, like the Jews, utterly rejected polytheism and longed for freedom from imperial domination, they were forming a new religious identity—or to put it another way, a new religious polity. They came to see themselves as the new Israel, the fulfillment of biblical prophecy, bound by a new covenant with the God of Israel, under which there would henceforth be no Jew and no Gentile (Gal. 3:28). This message, in particular, impacted the Gentiles of the Roman Empire, many of whom were converted to Christianity over a period of several centuries during which Christianity became the official religion of the Roman Empire. At the same time, the Jews as a body and their religious leaders insisted for the most part on fulfilling the commandments of the Torah as given and in reaffirming Jewish peoplehood.

The reception process with respect to the origins of Islam was understandably more complex. The first Muslims were not Jews but rather peninsular Arabs, fiercely iconoclastic, to whom Jews were certainly no strangers, and who were familiar with biblical traditions and postbiblical Judaism. Scholars have noted efforts to persuade the Jews of Arabia to join the Islamic monotheist polity, but as before, the main body of Jews in Arabia turned down the offer, so to speak, as did the majority of Jews elsewhere who came under Arab conquest. Once again, we encounter an ironic situation: the Jews, whose ancestral proclamation of the true God was being endorsed as a definitive tenet by yet another new religion are themselves rejected, or at the least restricted, for refusing to join that monotheist polity.

It is arguable that the emergence of Christianity in the first century C.E. was possible only because Israelite-Jewish monotheism had survived a series of "crises of faith," each of which might have broken the chain had it not been met successfully. It is my purpose here to trace these crises, which began in the Neo-Assyrian period, continued at intervals through the loss of both the Northern Israelite and Judean Kingdoms. The exiled Judeans endured separation from the homeland during the Babylonian and Egyptian exiles without a temple in Jerusalem. They overcame difficulties in reconstituting collective existence in the homeland during the Persian Period and subsequently

5

dealt with the religious and cultural challenges of Hellenism. In particular, the restoration of the cult of Yahweh in the Temple of Jerusalem by the Maccabees, who stood their ground against the religious persecutions of Antiochus IV in the second pre-Christian century, saved Jewish monotheism, whose continued existence was hanging by a thread. The very obstinacy, later attributed to the Jewish People by the heirs to their monotheist belief system, had earlier served to assure the survival of monotheism in late antiquity!

Monotheism in the Hebrew Bible: The Ascent of the Israelite God

The great historian, Arnold Toynbee, was fascinated by the fact that it was Yahweh, originally the tribal-national God of a numerically negligible, and in international terms, relatively powerless people, the ancient Israelites, that ultimately emerged as the universal God of a large part of humankind. How did this happen?

The short answer has already been posited: it was the consequence of the rise of Christianity as the official religion of the Roman Empire, later followed by the expansion of the Islamic polity over vast areas of the world. Both religions affirmed belief in the God of Abraham.

Searching for the long answer will take us back to the pre-Hellenistic period, to a discussion of the evolution of the Israelite-Jewish God idea and the factors that contributed to the survival of Judaism and of the Jewish people during what has been called the second commonwealth (or second temple period), preceding the advent of Hellenism in the late fourth century B.C.E. It is doubtful whether monotheism, as a belief system, would have survived at all if the Jewish collective endeavor in the homeland after the Exile had ended in failure. Christianity has recognized its debt to the heroic Maccabees, who took up arms in defense of Jewish monotheism, and thereby saved it, when it could have been lost to the ages. However, the debt to the restored Judean community of the Persian period has not been sufficiently acknowledged.

In the pre-Hellenistic period (from the late eight to the latter part of the fourth century B.C.E.), prophetic monotheism envisioned a world composed of many nations, who would abandon the idolatrous symbols of imperial power and unite in the belief that there is only one God, Yahweh, who alone rules over all nations. The Israelites, especially the Judean kings from Hezekiah and onward, are counseled to submit to Assyria, then Babylonia, and wait for Yahweh to bring down those evil empires. In this vision, Jerusalem was not slated to become the capital of a world empire, but rather to be the unique locus of oracular revelation, enabling conflicts among nations to be resolved without recourse to war (Isa. 2:2-4 // Mic. 4:1-3). We tend to forget that the fulfillment of the prophetic vision was to be international peace, not merely a universal theological confession.

These predicates represent remarkable responses, first to Assyrian, then to Neo-Babylonian imperial power. They demonstrate how the previously regional horizons of the Israelite prophets expanded to address an imperial world. The prophetic vision was introduced in the late eight century B.C.E. by First Isaiah (10:5-11, 14:24-27) and was endorsed a century later by Jeremiah (chaps. 25, 27). Whereas Sennacherib, the Assyrian, and Nebuchadnezzar II, the Babylonian, were Yahweh's instruments of punishment, Cyrus the Great, was to be the instrument of Israel's restoration, as proclaimed by Second Isaiah, during or soon after the Babylonian Exile (Isa. 45:1-7). Yet, the doctrine is the same: Yahweh rules over empires either way. What is new is the vital reinterpretation of First Isaiah and Jeremiah by the author of Second Isaiah that allowed for an exception to the predicted downfall of empires, more specifically, for an enabling role for the Achemenid empire. The restored Judean community endured and its territory was enlarged, all the while under far away Persian kings, not under a dynastic Davidite. Would this same community survive oncoming Hellenism, in general, and the religious persecutions of Antiochus IV, the Seleucid ruler, in particular?

Exile and Return: The Great Survival Challenge

The prophetic vision worked on two levels:

1. Acceptance of the prophetic policy of submission to empire by Hezekiah, King of Judah, ca. 701 B.C.E., and subsequently by Manasseh and the Judean leadership, enabled Judah to continue to exist, albeit weakened and at times in vassalage to Egypt, for about a century up until the final Babylonian destruction and the ensuing exile (587–586 B.C.E.).

2. The prophetic doctrine, as reinterpreted, legitimized the Judean restoration under Persian rulers, and a second temple was built on the very site of the first. Collectively, the Judeans were able to survive exile and to uphold strict monotheism in the process and then to operate successfully under a temple-centered system in Jerusalem. The restored Judean community, in what became known as Yehud, successfully parried divisive challenges by the Samaritans and adapted religious practice to the realities of a mixed society in the homeland. In the late fifth century B.C.E., what we now call *Judaism* emerged as an Israelite-based religious system, accommodated to the new facts on the ground, whereby sizable diaspora communities continued to "network" with the homeland.

There is now great attention being given to the Persian period (538–332 B.C.E.), which, until recently, had seemed to most scholars like a dark age. Our particular concern is in "survivability," on the assumption, already stated, that if the restored community had failed, or had totally assimilated, monotheism might not have survived. Our interest is, therefore, in the religious and social strategies of the restored community, where we encounter two distinguishable "voices," the one contractive and the other expansive. Once we get past issues involving the praxis of religion, the defining issue becomes that of boundaries: Who is a Jew, and who can become a Jew, and how so?

Was religious conversion as a transformative act, such as was practiced in Judaism of the Greco-Roman period and beyond, operative in pre-Hellenistic times? Some have inferred from Ezra, chapters 9 and 10, echoed in Nehemiah (13:1-3), that it was not. There we read of efforts to cleanse the restored Judean community of intermarriage. As Ezra tells it, the Judean returnees, including their leaders and sons, had taken to marrying the daughters of "the peoples of the land," whose practices were as abominable as those of the "peoples" of Canaan, with whom the Israelites had been forbidden to marry when they first entered Canaan, according to Deuteronomy (7:1-11). This practice is repeatedly referred to in Ezra as 'the sacrilege of the exiles," namely, of the returning exiles. It has been argued that if formal conversion had been operational at the time, there would have been an obvious remedy available to the zealous among the religious leadership of the returnees, an alternative to the disruptive and cruel banishment of foreign wives. These wives could have simply been converted to Israelite-Jewish religion.

The fact is that the entire episode of the banishment of foreign wives appears to go against long-term biblical policies on marriage with non-Israelite women. Most societies require periodic input from the outside, especially after wars, migrations, and natural disasters, and the biblical narrative describes, and its laws prescribe, procedures to that end. Strict endogamy was actually rare, so that the tone of Ezra, chapters 9 and 10, sounds like an ephemeral reaction to an emergency situation, rather than a long-term religious policy. The leaders of the returnees were examining genealogies and accrediting legitimate priests.

However understood, the Ezra-Nehemiah sources represent only one voice. Other biblical references, unfortunately of a cryptic nature, indicate that Israelite-Jewish religion, turned "Judaism," welcomed and, in fact, gained new adherents during and after the Babylonian Exile. We begin with the story of Ruth, the Moabite woman, which dates from sometime between the onset of exile and the early post-exilic period. Here is her declaration to Naomi, her Judean mother-in-law (Ruth 1:16-17):

> Then Ruth said: "Do not urge me to leave you and to turn
> back from following you; for wherever you go I will go, and

wherever you lodge I will lodge. Your kinfolk (or: "people")
shall be my kinfolk (or: "people"), and your God shall be
my God. Wherever you die I will die, and there shall I be
buried. So much may Yahweh do to me and even more, if
anything but death ever separates between me and you.

This statement sounds like an act of conversion, and certain Jewish
traditions understood it as such. It projects identity on three levels:
Ruth would worship Naomi's God, join her people, and live and die in
her mother-in-law's land. The declaration lends to Ruth's commitment
a quasi-ritual quality, because it includes an imprecation in the name of
Yahweh. What we have is the story of a young widow from Moab who,
defying custom, comes to live in the land of Judah with her mother-
in-law instead of returning to her Moabite family after the death of her
husband. In that situation, Ruth would, as expected in ancient Near
Eastern societies, assume the religion of her adoptive family and revere
the God of her new land. Her Judean family relative and husband des-
ignate, Boaz, shows her kindness and protects her, while characterizing
her decision as the act of one seeking haven under the protection of
Yahweh. Ruth was welcomed in Judah, and her narrative epitomizes
friendly feelings towards erstwhile enemies.

We read in several exilic and early post-exilic sources about groups
of non-Israelites who had attached themselves to Yahweh (the Niphᶜal
form *nilwāh*) during the Exile and at periods of return. The notion of
attachment originates in Jeremiah (50:4-5), where it refers to Judah
and Israel themselves who had become estranged from Yahweh, and
who now sought reattachment:

In those days and at that time, speech of Yahweh, the sons of
Israel, they and the sons of Judah together, will continuously
weep as they go, and will seek Yahweh, their God. They will
inquire of Zion, directing their advance there: "Come, let us
attach ourselves (read: *wenillāweh*) to Yahweh in an everlast-
ing covenant that shall not be forgotten."

This theme is reused by prophets of the Exile and return. Thus, Third Isaiah (Isa. 56: 3):

> "Furthermore, let not the foreigner who was attached (*hannilwāh*) to Yahweh say: 'Yahweh will surely separate me from his people."

Resuming in Isaiah 56: 6–8, we read the words of Yahweh:

> As for the foreigners who are attached (*hannilwîm*) to Yahweh, to serve him and to love the name of Yahweh, to become his servants—all who observe the Sabbath and do not profane it, and who fulfill my covenant—I will bring them to my sacred mountain, and let them celebrate in my house of prayer. Their burnt offerings and sacrifices shall be acceptable on my altar, for my House shall be known as a house of prayer for all peoples. Speech of the Lord, God, who gathers in the dispersed of Israel. [I will yet gather more of him (= of Israel) in addition to those of him (=Israel) already gathered.]

Similarly, in First Zechariah (2:14–15a):

> Shout for joy, daughter Zion! For behold, I am coming; and I will dwell in your midst, speech of Yahweh. And many nations will become attached (*wenilwû*) to Yahweh on that day, and they shall be to me as a people. I will dwell in your midst. (cf. Isa. 14:1, Jer. 50:5)

We know very little about the infrequent Hebrew verb *l-w-h*. It can refer to a military alliance whereby armies "join" with other forces in battle, (Ps. 83:9, and cf. Esther 9:27), as well as to other formal associations. In the first, brief statement in Third-Isaiah, the anxious *nilwîm* are reassured that Yahweh will not sever the bond that had been formed between them and "my people;" that they will be restored along with the Judeans. They will not be cast out of the reconstituted Judean community. The elaborative statement that follows, with its likely interpolation, defines the status of the "attached" more clearly. They are non-Israelites who commit to serving Yahweh out of love for his name, such service being specified as observance of the Sabbath and fulfillment of the covenant. On this basis, they will be welcome to worship in Yahweh's restored Temple, which is open to all peoples. These specifications indicate that the persons in question would participate in the religious life of the Jewish community. The statement in First Zechariah closes the circle by prophesying that nations of *nilwîm* will be "to me as a people," which is to say, like Jews. This sounds like conversion, though we note the absence of reference to a rite, such as circumcision, that would signify Jewish identity. Such may be alluded to, however, in the reference to fulfillment of Yahweh's *berît*, "covenant" as a prerequisite of acceptance.

Somewhere in this mix belongs a passage in First Kings, chapter 8, a multilayered text that narrates the dedication of Solomon's Temple in Zion/Jerusalem, when the ark was deposited in the inner sanctum. In its final form, chapter 8 resonates with Second Samuel, chapter 7, the dynastic covenant with the house of David, which is Deuteronomist in tone. In other respects, it employs language and projects images characteristic of priestly sources, suggesting that it is relatively late; a product of the very postexilic period that interests us here. It includes a prayer that is informative for our present discussion. The chapter may be outlined as follows:

> 8:1-11: An account, adapted by the priests, of the installation of the ark in the Temple.
>
> 8:12-13: A royal proclamation on the intended function of the Temple as an earthly residence for a deity who dwells in a celestial cloud-envelope. This is the earliest, core statement in chapter 8.
>
> 8:14-21: A blessing by Solomon that resonates with Second Samuel, chapter 7, and confirms the acceptability of the Temple project in Jerusalem.

8:22-53: A lengthy prayer, once again with Deuteronomist overtones and priestly diction, that outlines the expiatory functions of the Temple as the sanctified locus of sacrifice and joyous prayer. Focus here is on 8:41–43, an invitation to the non-Israelite foreigner to worship in the Temple. This is probably an even later addition to the already late prayer.

8:54-66: The consecration of the Temple, celebrated with sacrifice, blessings, and prayers, in which universal monotheism is proclaimed, and the very existence of other gods firmly denied (v. 60).

Verses 41-43 are central to our discussion. They read as follows:

> And as well, with respect to the foreigner (*hannokrî*), who is, himself, not of your people, Israel, who comes from a distant land for the purpose of honoring your name—where they have heard of your great name, and your strong hand and your outstretched arm—and has directed prayers to this house: May you hear in heaven, at the throne where you are seated, and perform all that the foreigner may call upon you to do. This is so that all the peoples of the earth may acknowledge your name, to worship you as your people Israel do, and to acknowledge that your name is proclaimed over this house which I have built.

In reading this section of the prayer one is reminded of the story of Jonah, where we find diverse, non-Israelite seafarers aboard a storm-tossed ship on the way to Tarshish, calling out to Yahweh, Jonah's God, after their own gods had failed to quell the storm. Significantly, they pledge votives and sacrifices to the God of Israel, whose unique power over earth, heaven and sea, they now acknowledge (Jon. 1:14-15). Presumably, their offerings would be acceptable.

It seems that the authors of this prayer (and of the book of Jonah) were cognizant of an attraction to Israelite religion, turned Judaism, perhaps nurtured by Israel's success in reconstituting its national life in the homeland. This mentality is reflected in First Zechariah (8:20-23), where the prophet foresees many peoples coming to Jerusalem to seek the presence of Yahweh of Hosts and to bring their petitions before him.

It is worth mentioning that the priestly Pesah (=Passover) code of Exodus 12 (verses 43-50) provides no remedy for the foreigner (*ben nēkār*) that would have allowed him to celebrate the festival, as the same code does with respect to the *gēr*, "alien resident," who may celebrate upon being circumcised. In Solomon's prayer, the foreigner celebrates the cult, though there is nothing said about a requirement of circumcision. However, the absence of a reference to circumcision may be a matter of genre; a prayer such as this is not likely to prescribe a particular ritual requirement. Yet, the difference with respect to the *nokrî* is significant. Something has changed; in effect, the foreigner is also welcomed.

Now, both the prayer and the code emanate from the priestly establishment of the postexilic, Achemenid period, and one would expect them both to reflect priestly policy of that period. The hidden agenda of both texts is religious conversion. Exodus 12:43-50 is best understood as legislating ritual conversion with circumcision, but only for those, like the *gēr*, who are long-term residents of Israelite-Jewish communities. The narrative of Genesis, chapter 34, pertaining to the rape of Dinah, of priestly provenance, likewise alludes to conversion. The Shechemites offer Jacob and his clan the privileges of residence in Canaan, including intermarriage. Jacob's sons assent on condition that the men of Shechem undergo circumcision, a condition that the Shechemites accept. This demand was a ruse, but it presupposes operative conversion with circumcision. First Kings 8, indicates a broadening of the range to include those less familiar to the Israelite-Jewish society. Conceivably, it is directed at non-Jews residing in proximity to diaspora communities, rather than only to those in the homeland. It is relevant, in any case, to mention that in traditional Judaism the term for "proselyte" is, in fact, *gēr*. We are not informed whether the Jewish leadership during the Persian period actively sought out non-Jews in an effort to convert them.

Before we leave the Persian period, during which prophecy ceased, it is important to recognize that prophetic characterizations of the divine plan had left certain issues unclear, so that the political agenda of prophetic universalism remains elusive. In addition to foreseeing the downfall of evil empires and the enlistment of a more friendly empire in Israel's restoration, did the Israelite-Jewish prophets ever envisage the conversion of the Gentiles, in the sense that they would all become Israelites/Jews? What was to be the status of the nations of the world, of those, for example, who would flock to Zion to receive oracular instruction from Yahweh, as predicted in First Isaiah, chapter 2 and Micah, chapter 4?

The prophetic vision, from First Isaiah on, projects a supranational, or extranational "cosmo-polity," that would operate with a new concept of spiritual, rather than military or political power. This polity would include the nations of the world, who would retain their erstwhile identity but would cast off their idols and honor the God of Israel and his people.

Challenges of the Greco-Roman Period

As the power of the Persian Empire in the Near East waned in the mid-to-late fourth century B.C.E., and Greek power rose, the reinterpretation of the prophetic vision that had legitimized Persian imperial rule over homeland Jewry took on a new urgency. Now, the Jews of the homeland were to behold the demise of yet another empire. Would the prophetic vision and its doctrine of submission to empire prove credible in the Hellenistic age, when the Ptolemies of Egypt and the Seleucids of Syria were to rule Palestine and when Roman power in the region was on the rise? We are actually speaking of two related challenges: (1) Hellenization, a broad cultural process with religious and political ramifications that continued over time, and (2) the Maccabean rebellion against Antiochus IV (167–164 B.C.E.) that succeeded in restoring the Yahwist cult to the temple of Jerusalem and achieved limited political independence until 63 B.C.E., when the Romans entered Jerusalem.

It has often been noted that the Greeks were different from other ancient Near Eastern conquerors, whose wars were conventionally aimed at empire-building—at territorial expansion, wealth, and the collection of tribute and the imposition of vassalage. Not so the Greeks, who brought something more to conquest. Possessed of a sense of cultural superiority and nurtured by philosophers such as Aristotle, Alexander the Great and the Greek conquerors who followed him actively sought to bring their language and culture to conquered lands, and when we speak of Greek culture and society we inevitably include religion as an endemic feature. The many peoples living within the orbit of Greek civilization were being offered an almost irresistible opportunity. Yet, for the Jewish community of Palestine, and for Jewish diaspora communities like those in Egypt, the religious concomitants of Hellenization posed a particular set of challenges, affecting Judaism's monotheist cult and threatening fidelity to the Torah as the authoritative Jewish text.

The Hellenistic period, especially the Maccabean episode, have been studied in great depth by scholars, who have been able to unravel the shifting rivalries within the contemporary Jewish community of Jerusalem and the homeland and to describe some of its major accommodations to Hellenism. Under the Ptolemies and Seleucids, up to and including the reign of Antiochus III, imperial policy was to continue regarding the cult of Yahweh in the Jerusalem temple as inviolate. Amidst flagrant internal Jewish contention over the high priesthood and other forms of internecine manipulation, the monotheism of Jerusalem's Jews, though subject to compromise, survived. Some Jewish factions seem to have been overly eager to accommodate Hellenizing pressures, and we don't know how far such tendencies might have gone. Official toleration came to an end, however, when Antiochus IV, restorer of the Seleucid Empire, demanded direct allegiance to the imperial, pagan cult after declaring Jerusalem to be part of an Antiochene Republic, which he headed. The Jerusalem Temple was desecrated, the observance of the Jewish festivals banned, and the cult of Yahweh suspended for about three and one half years. These religious persecutions crossed the line, not only for deeply pious Jews, but for those aroused by an activist priestly family, that of Mattathias of Modi'in.

The Maccabean rebellion, soon to be led by Mattathias's son, Judah, and subsequently by other members of that priestly family, succeeded in a series of battles over several years to regain control of the Temple and to restore the Yahwist cult in Jerusalem, free of idolatrous features. This period is recorded and evaluated in First and Second Maccabees and in other ancient sources, such as the histories of Josephus Flavius. A new holiday, Hanukkah, was declared to commemorate this rededication—it was originally called "Sukkoth of the month of Kislev."

Ultimately, Palestinian Jewry had to settle for much less than full independence, but Jewish monotheism was safe for the while. In the process, it had become clear that the prophetic doctrine of submission to empire would not work under the unprecedented conditions of religious coercion; that without an operational Jewish cult in the Temple of Jerusalem, the Jews of Palestine might have lost their identity. In the period from 164 B.C.E., when the Maccabean revolt ended, to 63 B.C.E., when Rome conquered Jerusalem, Hasmonean kings governed. Under the Romans, Jewish kings continued to govern under special arrangements affecting the temple cult. Instead of worshiping emperors, Jews prayed for the welfare of the emperor and the empire. This situation, with intermittent rumblings, continued until the Roman destruction of Jerusalem and its Temple in 70 B.C.E.

In the context of the present discussion, interest lies in the contemporary character of Jewish religion and culture and in its responses to Hellenism and imperial domination. We note the proliferation of largely apocalyptic sects, now better known from the Dead Sea Scrolls, some of them evidencing considerable Hellenization. As has been shown, this trend was also characteristic of the Hasmonean and post-Hasmonean kings. Of special interest is an instance of collective conversion, that of the sometimes hostile Edomites (=Idumeans) to the south, by the expansionist Hasmonean king, John Hyrcanus. There is some doubt as to whether such conversion was fully coerced, but regardless, this episode attests to the contemporary practice of conversion and represents a Jewish petty-king acting in the manner of a Greek conqueror, only pressing Judaism, not Hellenism.

We cannot leave the second pre-Christian century without discussing two literary monuments, the Wisdom of Jeshua Ben Sirach and the Book of Daniel, both products of this period. The Wisdom of Ben Sirach was written in Hebrew by a single author in the first quarter of the second century B.C.E.. It represents an affirmation of Judaism and of Jewish history by a Jewish sage who had come to terms with the challenge of Hellenism during a brief period of stability under the Ptolemies, then the Seleucids, prior to the persecutions of Antiochus IV. It resonates with the biblical Book of Proverbs and with other wisdom sources. What is of particular interest in the context of the present discussion is Ben Sirach's section beginning with chapter 44 and continuing to near the end of the book, where the Sage praises Israel's ancestors. Within that framework, his "take" on two worthy kings of Judah, Hezekiah, and Josiah (Sirach 48:15–49:13), is especially noteworthy. Hezekiah heeded the prophet Isaiah, who counseled submission to Sennacherib, the Assyrian, and Jerusalem was saved. The last kings of Judah failed to heed Jeremiah (even though Josiah, for his part, was righteous), and consequently the Kingdom of Judah came to an end. Ben Sirach may well have understood the political vision of the Israelite prophets, although his confidence in accommodation would soon prove to have been misplaced.

The Book of Daniel preserves a collection of apocalyptic visions that depict the God of Israel and his angels, first empowering and then bringing down kings and empires according to a schedule of cut-off times, ending in the long-awaited redemption of Israel in its land. The Book of Daniel shows an awareness of the religious persecutions under Antiochus IV, but it cannot be clearly identified by its content with any of the otherwise known Jewish factions. Whereas it praises firm devotion to the God of Israel, it knows nothing of armed Jewish resistance. The stated proponents of the visions in Daniel are the *maśkîlîm,* "the enlightened," who claim to understand Yahweh's final plan (Dan. 1:4, 11:35, 12:3, 10). In the context of the present discussion, the apocalypse of Daniel is best understood as an alternative to the Maccabean response to the religious persecutions of Antiochus IV. Its authors were watching the changing fortunes of the Seleucids, looking for signals that the God of Israel is bringing down yet another empire, thereby enabling Israel's redemption. Indeed, the Seleucid Empire fell, but, it was not to be the last empire. Rome was to follow.

The advent of Christianity in Roman Palestine was only one among several transformations encountered by contemporary Jewry, foremost among them the destruction of the Jerusalem temple and mass exile. As affects religious identity, the Jews would no longer remain the only monotheists. The exclusivity characteristic of monotheism as a belief system was about to take aim at new targets and turn in new directions over a period of centuries, when Islam would later become the third member of the monotheist club.

Is There a Way Out? A Jewish Agenda for Cooperating Monotheisms

As heir to Israelite religion, Judaism has been and remains capable of accommodation to changing circumstances affecting the collective existence of the Jewish People, who were sustained by a universal, prophetic vision that continued to give them hope. This vision portrays the redeemed world as one of peace among all nations and freedom from tyranny. An agenda for the actualization of this vision is preserved in the traditional Jewish liturgy for the High Holy Days, Rosh Hashanah and Yom Kippur, where we find a series of petitions brought before the God of Israel. Following ancient blessings that affirm the Lord's identity as the God of Abraham, who sustains the living and resurrects the dead and who is the sacred Sovereign of the universe, the following prayers are customarily recited:

(a) Therefore, instill the awe of you, oh Lord our God, over all your works,
And fear of you over all whom you have created;
So that all the works shall fear you,
And all those created shall bow down before you.
Let them all compose themselves into one band,
To do your will with a whole heart.
For we acknowledge, oh Lord, our God, that sovereignty is yours;
Might is in your arm,
And triumph in your right arm,
And your name is awesome over all you have created.

(b) Therefore, grant honor, oh Lord, to your people,
Praise to those who fear you,
Abundant hope to those who seek you;
And grant access to those who look hopefully to you.
Joy to your land, and gladness to your city;
Increased strength to David, your servant,
And a "rekindling of light" to the son of Jesse, your anointed one.

(c) Therefore, the righteous shall rejoice at what they behold;
And the upright shall exult,
And the devout shall delight in song.
Wrongdoing shall be silenced,
And all wickedness, all of it, shall dispel like smoke;
When you eliminate the Empire of Evil from the earth.

(d) Then, shall you rule; you, oh Lord, over all your works,
On Mount Zion, abode of your glorious presence,
And in Jerusalem, your holy city.
As it is written in your sacred words:
"The Lord shall reign forever; your God, Zion, for all generations."
  (Ps.146:10)

Commentary

(a) Given that it is God's will that all humans unite to worship God, we ask God to instill in us the will to do his will. We acknowledge that all power is God's, and that God's sovereignty over creation ought to be universally affirmed. We recognize, however, that this can eventuate only when humankind acts in consort to achieve it; when the nations of the world are at peace. There is no specific reference to the Jewish People in this part of the prayer; the point of departure is individual, and the horizon is universal. The prayer does not envision the dissolution of the nations of the world or expect that all people will become Jews. The thematic word is Hebrew *ma'asîm,* "works"; all who were created by God shall serve God.

This prayer resonates with the prophetic vision of international peace in Isaiah 2 (// Micah 4). Isaiah predicts that many peoples will realize that God is both powerful and just and, accordingly, will direct their gaze to the Temple Mount in Jerusalem, where they will be instructed by God on how to resolve their conflicts without resort to war. The author of this prayer exhibits a different perspective, focusing on what must evolve before the human quest for divine guidance can succeed. Humankind requests God's help in achieving the unity that has thus far eluded the world.

(b) In this part of the prayer, the focus shifts to Israel's destiny. God is petitioned to grant his people, Israel, an honored place in the family of nations, free and sovereign in God's country and rejoicing in Jerusalem, God's holy city. The "beginning of redemption," has been realized in the modern State of Israel, home to more than one-third of the Jewish people, who speak Hebrew, the revived and modernized tongue of the prophets. The independence of The State of Israel (also known as "The State of the Jewish People") was declared less than a decade after one-third of world Jewry had perished in the holocaust.

What earlier Jews had been pleading with God to do over the centuries, some modern Jews, operating with a concept of "auto-emancipation," undertook to do on their own initiative, and they succeeded dramatically. The image of the Davidic Messiah was taken by early Zionists to symbolize the Jewish restoration to the biblical homeland as a free people. To modulate a biblical dictum: God observed all that his sons and daughters had done, and saw that it was good, and he blessed it. To advance the redemption of Israel, the present challenge for Israel is to negotiate peace with the Palestinians and with neighboring nations, most of whom are Muslim, and hence monotheist.

(c) The prayer returns to global concerns, originally referring to the hoped-for downfall of the Roman Empire, but applicable to the evils of imperialism in every age. We pray for the end of tyranny, when all those who have kept the faith will have cause to rejoice. Once again, there is no specific reference to the People of Israel; the end of political evil is to be total and global, vindicating all of the righteous.

(d) Only when all of the above come to pass will the sovereignty of Zion's God over the human world be universally affirmed.

So we ask: Who holds the rights to the one, true God?

Answer: All who worship him sincerely, as it is written: "The Lord is near to all his 'callers'; to all who call upon him truthfully" (Ps. 145:18).

In Depth: Recommended Sources for Further Study

The work of Francis E. Peters has been most helpful in understanding the historic relationship between the three monotheist religions. He analyzes how classical texts, often the same texts, were interpreted differently in each religious tradition, noting progressive differences within each tradition. In effect, he gives us the very kind of dialogue that we have been looking for, illustrating how the texts talk to each other. See Francis E. Peters, *Judaism, Christianity and Islam: The Classical Texts and Their Interpretation.* 3 vols. (Princeton, NJ: Princeton University Press, 1990). Also by the same author: *The Monotheists: Jews, Christians, and Muslims in Conflict and Competition.* 2 vols. (Princeton, NJ: Princeton University Press, 1994). Professor Peters summarizes his views in *Children of Abraham: Judaism, Christianity and Islam* (Princeton, NJ: Princeton University Press, 2004). For a concise treatment of aspects of this subject see Sidney H. Griffith, "The Bible and the 'People of the Book.'" *Bulletin, DEI VERBUM, Catholic Biblical Association* 79–80, English ed. (2006): 22–30.

For concessionary statements on the survival of the Jews and Judaism by a highly skeptical historian, see: Arnold J. Toynbee, *A Study of History*, abridg. of vols. I–VI by D. C. Somervell (New York: Oxford University Press, 1946), 135–139, 475, 500 ff., 523–5.

I have recently proposed a hypothesis on the early development of Israelite monotheism that finds in the Hebrew Bible responses to political and military challenges that threatened the credibility of Israel's faith. See Baruch A. Levine, "Assyrian Ideology and Israelite Monotheism," in *NINEVEH: Papers of the XLIXe Rencontre Assyriologique Internationale*, ed. D. Colon and A. George (*Iraq* 67), (British School of Archaeology in Iraq, 2005), 2:411–27; reprinted in: *In Search of Meaning: Collected Studies of Baruch A. Levine*, ed. Andrew D. Gross, vol. I, (Winona Lake IN: Eisenbrauns, 2011), 3–28.

We are fortunate in having a monumental history of the Persian Empire which covers the Achemenid period in great detail and with penetrating analysis. See: Pierre Briant, *From Cyrus to Alexander: A History of the Persian Empire*, trans. Peter T. Daniels (Winona Lake, IN: Eisenbrauns, 2002). More directly addressing problems in biblical history are studies by Oded Lipschits and his circle. See Oded Lipschits, *The Fall and Rise of Jerusalem: Judah under Babylonian Rule* (Winona Lake, IN: Eisenbrauns, 2005). Also Oded Lipschits, Gary N. Knoppers, Rainer Albertz, eds. *Judah and the Judeans in the Fourth Century B.C.E,* (Winona Lake, IN: Eisenbrauns, 2007).

An in-depth study of the Maccabean period and of Jerusalem under the Ptolemies and Seleucidsj is provided by Jonathan A. Goldstein in his introduction to "I Maccabees," in *The Anchor Bible* (Garden City, NY: Doubleday, 1976). Especially note: "What Really Happened: The Civic and Religious Policies of Antiochus IV," with chronological table, 104–74.

Do Monotheist Religions Worship the Same God? A Perspective on Classical Judaism

Jacob Neusner

I. Verisimilitude versus Authenticity: A Philosophical Question Addressed to a Revealed Historical Religion

The issue of verisimilitude versus authenticity need not detain us very long. Because things look alike, they are not necessarily alike—the same thing. Judaism, Christianity, and Islam, the monotheist religions, concur on one principle: not all religions that declare God one are the same. The task is to evaluate the differences in proportion and in context: to test the probative value of verisimilitude. We carry out the test by asking one monotheist religion its opinion of another monotheist religion: Does it discern the similarities that appear obvious to us as outsiders? Let me start from the beginning: how we compare religions. I begin with the paradox of asking philosophical questions of historical data: generalizing out of detail. When we speak of monotheist religions we invoke *isms*—categories of generalization, philosophy, applied logic, and practical reason that sustain generalization. But we find our data in the details—the legal and exegetical, narrative canon of those religions.

Rabbinic Judaism in its formative statements pursued philosophical problems about types of causation and the many and the one, for example. But it solved those problems through the analysis of cases and the provision of probative examples, leaving it to later generations to articulate the system implicit in the cases. Here, therefore, we raise a philosophical question about God in general. To respond to the question we draw upon the particular narrative canon in all its specificity.

"Monotheism" generalizes about the nature of God and speaks of the oneness, the unity, the uniqueness of God—all of them philosophical categories susceptible of critical generalization and logical analysis. But when we wish to speak of classical Judaism, we turn to its ancient canon of Scripture and Rabbinic tradition, and that tradition does not frame its conceptions in abstraction and generalization. The Judaic canon is made up first by prophecy and narrative and the exegesis of narrative and second by laws in all their specificity and the need to generalize about cases. Now there is no such thing as *religion in general.* But we pursue the conception of *God in general.*

Philosophy of religion in general contrasts with theology *of a religion.* A philosophical formulation responds out of a comprehensive logic, producing abstract generalizations concerning the nature of religion. A religious counterpart in theology responds out of the revealed truths of a necessarily singular tradition. The former seeks to generalize data into comprehensive reason, the latter to particularize the question and to answer it out of a body of revealed truth. Philosophy establishes truth-claims out of diverse data through criticism and practical logic and reason. Religious truth-claims based on a priori affirmations of truth and facts establish for themselves a position exempt from criticism and beyond the reach of reason. Such ready-made formulations as "this we believe" or "so we affirm" suffice to prove the point in the context of a revealed religion but shut off discussion in the setting of reason and philosophy of religion.

II. Do Monotheist Religions Worship the Same God?

By their own word all monotheist religions—religions that define the omnipotent and universal God they worship as singular, unique, and manifestly one and not many beings or entities—worship the one and the same God. For when they speak of the monotheist God, that affirmation extends to all those who concur on the normative and indicative traits of "God in general." That is why monotheist philosophers of religion—Judaic, Christian, Islamic—in medieval times could find it possible to engage in a common debate. They concur on the same language of abstract definition and on some of the same scriptural and narrative traditions and share the same categories for the description of the one God they affirm. Not only so, but these categories derive from a logic in common concerning what that God is and does. If I affirm that by "God" I mean *a unique omnipotent being, just and merciful* and you affirm that by "God" you mean a unique omnipotent being with the same traits, then it follows that we concur in our respective accounts of the same being that we call by the same name and classify by the same traits. Each party speaks of God in a manner consistent with the other—a sharing of convictions. At the end I shall offer that affirmation in common as the foundation of interfaith dialogue, the possibility of debate on a common agendum.

Monotheist philosophy begins where religion (including theology) ends. Addressing a mass of data, it formulates an abstraction out of the resources of logic, along the lines of the following: "If there should be a monotheist God, of what would his definition consist?" Religion concludes in the following rejoinder: "Since God revealed himself to the prophet, there is no *if* but only an established given," a *since*, that is, an established set of a priori facts. Monotheist religion thus frames a concrete doctrine out of the canonical writings it knows beyond all criticism to be true. But monotheist philosophers—systematic and critical—then pursue the logic of those revealed truths and facts. That is what I meant when I said philosophy begins where religion ends: philosophy takes up the revealed truths of religion and seeks to extend the results of revelation, to uncover what is implicit and to test the outcome against applied reason and practical logic.

Now that I have outlined what I conceive to be the two approaches, philosophical and generalizing, theological and particularizing, I take up the generative question. That is, do the monotheist religions worship the same God? Let me turn to the response of a particular religion, in all its specificity, in its classical canon, the one on which I work. How do we respond out of the resources of classical Judaism? What we shall see is a rejection of the logic outlined just now, the logic that treats resemblance as proof.

Monotheistic religions resemble one another in maintaining the unity of God, therefore monotheist religions ought to be construed to worship the same God. That would be true only if the particular monotheist tradition recognizes the religions that resemble monotheisms as monotheistic. We now ask Rabbinic Judaism in its classical canon whether it recognizes Christianity as resembling itself.

III. The Perspective of Classical Judaism: The Status of the *Minim*, Who Possess the Same Scriptures as Israel and Are Like Israel

I turn to the question: *On what grounds does normative Judaism claim that its monotheism encompasses all monotheisms, so that Judaic faithful worship the same God as Christians or Islamists worship?*

In its classical sources, normative Judaism does not recognize any other religion as monotheistic like itself and any other people as the same thing as holy Israel—the people of the *Shema*, "Hear Israel the Lord our God is the one God." The question addressed to normative Judaism, in its formative age, finds its response in the canon of that Judaism, consisting of Scripture and the Rabbinic documents from the Mishnah through the second Talmud, ca. 200–600, that extend

Scripture. But those sources do not explicitly reply to that question. The problem is not only that Islam begins after the closure of the formative stage of the Rabbinic canon. Judaism in its formative age makes no comment on Islam. The problem is that normative Judaism does not recognize the truth or even the existence of *any* other religion. By that I mean classical Judaism does not engage with the truth-claims of any other religious system. No other religion qualifies as monotheist, for by definition and by analysis none can. Integral to true monotheism is the source of truth, which is the revealed Torah of Sinai. Israel is authentic by reason of the Torah, and Israel uniquely possesses the Torah. So Islam later on differs not at all from Christianity earlier.

The normative legal sources accordingly take for granted that Judaism is the only true religion. The law recognizes the claim of another religious tradition to inherit the Torah and rejects that claim. When confusing verisimilitude with authenticity Christianity is portrayed as both like and not like Judaism. It resembles Judaism only in part. But it replicates its truth not at all. It is characterized in the following language:

Tosefta Shabbat 13:5

A. The books of the Evangelists and the books of the *minim* they do not save from a fire [on the Sabbath]. But they are allowed to burn where they are,

B. they and the references to the Divine Name that are in them.

C. R. Yosé the Galilean says, "On ordinary days, one cuts out the references to the Divine Name which are in them and stores them away, and the rest burns."

D. Said R. Tarfon, "May I bury my sons, if such things come into my hands and I do not burn them, and even the references to the Divine Name that are in them.

E. "And if someone was running after me, I should go into a temple of idolatry, but I should not go into their houses [of worship].

F. "For idolaters do not recognize the Divinity in denying him, but these recognize the Divinity and deny him.

G. "And about them Scripture states, 'Behind the door and the doorpost you have set up your symbol for deserting me, you have uncovered your bed' (Isa. 57:8)."

H. Said R. Ishmael, "Now if to bring peace between a man and his wife, the Omnipresent declared that a scroll written in a state of sanctification should be blotted out by water, the books of the *minim*, which bring enmity between Israel and their Father who is in heaven, all the more so should be blotted out,

I. "they and the references to the Divine Name in them.

J. "And concerning them has Scripture stated, 'Do I not hate them that hate thee, O Lord? And do I not loathe them that rise up against thee? I hate them with perfect hatred, I count them my enemies' (Ps. 139:21-22)."

K. Just as they do not save them on account of fire, so they do not save them from a ruin, or a flood, or anything that will turn them to rubble.

The issue is how in case of fire to deal with books of *minim* on the Sabbath (the word *minim* bears the use and meaning of "sectarian"). Scrolls of the Torah are saved from fire on the Sabbath, even though one is not permitted otherwise to handle fire on the Sabbath. The *minim* possess scrolls in which are incised the divine name. Because they belong to *minim*, they are left to burn. Possession by *minim* or (in context) other idolaters disqualifies the scroll and removes its sacred status. The formulation of the issue thus presupposes that the scrolls are holy but the disposition of the case denies that holiness by reason of the *min's* ownership of them. So the *minim*—no different from idolaters—affect the standing of the object that is possessed. The *minim* exercise the power of sanctification. But so do idolaters.

Who are those in a class of outsiders but other than that of idolaters? They are persons who share the same canon as is held by the Rabbis, for the law takes for granted we deal with scrolls deemed sacred by Israelites. Otherwise there is no issue. On the margins of Israelite society, the *minim* clearly belong to non-Israel, since their ownership of the scrolls disqualifies the otherwise valid holy scrolls. That precipitates the problem before us: the ambiguous status of the scrolls, which are like Israel's scrolls in their contents but not like Israel in their circumstance.

Two positions contend. First, we recognize the sanctity of the scrolls and rescue them from a fire even on the Sabbath, because the character of the scrolls, their contents, not the circumstance of who owns them, settles the question. Second, we ignore the indicators of sanctification in the scrolls and invoke the criterion of circumstance, ownership by nonbelievers. That right of ownership nullifies the sanctity of the scrolls including the representations of the divine name incised in them.

We now ask our particular question: In the conception of the Rabbinic canon portrayed by the Tosefta, do the *minim* worship the same God as does normative Judaism represented by the Rabbinic canon? This question is answered in so many words: they know but deny. By their own action, in possessing canonical documents, the *minim* mark themselves as Israelites. And this is made explicit, for the authentic idolaters do not recognize the Divinity in denying him, but these marginal people recognize the Divinity and deny him. It is a spiteful act of denial of what authentic Israel affirms.

We thus address a sector of Israel, not the idolater, for the idolater is not represented as spiteful, the *min* is. We furthermore acknowledge the Israel-ness of the *minim*, because our ruling concedes their power to define the status of the Torah-scrolls. The fact that they own them suffices implicitly to resolve the conflict between governing considerations, contents versus circumstance.

Idolaters and *minim* possess the power to resolve the ambiguity of status involved in the case of holy scrolls owned by unholy persons. Their owners' attitudes register and dictate the standing of the scrolls subject to their attitude. This brings us to the heart of the matter. The Rabbinic laws regard the pagan and the *min* as possessing the power

31

of intentionality to define the standing of Scriptures for the *min* or of idols for the idolater. So the *min* and the idolater categorically differ but correspond. This classic case of verisimilitude versus authenticity is made explicit in the law:

Mishnah Abodah Zarah 3:4-5

3:4 F.   It is said only, ". . . their gods" (Deut. 12:3)—that which one treats as a god is prohibited, but that which one treats not as a god is permitted.

3:5 E.   On what account is an "asherah" prohibited? Because it has been subject to manual labor, and whatever had been subject to manual labor is prohibited.

The fact that the Gentile treated the object as a god and subjected it to manual labor assigns to it the status of a god—has sanctified the object. That brings us back to the main point: *the minim possess the power to sanctify the scrolls.* Does that mean they worship the same God as the Israelites? No, it does not. The actions of the *minim* are comparable in effect to the actions of the idolaters. Idolaters and *minim* do not believe in the same God as the Israelites. Yes, the *min* or idolater has the power to effect the sanctification of the object. No, the *min* does not worship the one true God. His marginal status assigns him a place in Israel but not a secure place.

We now revert to and answer the four basic questions:

• Does classical Judaism believe that Jews and Gentiles and *minim* worship the same God? The Gentiles are idolaters and worship sticks and stones. The *minim* by contrast possess the Torah, but they have taken the path of apostasy away from the God of Israel. They worship the same God as do the Israelites but do so in a flawed manner.

• On what basis do the Rabbinic laws make the judgment that they make? They acknowledge the Israelite scriptures, but err in their reading of those Scriptures so that that recognition imposes the status of heretic on the *min*.

• What conditions must be satisfied for us to say that Jews and Christians worship the same God? Christians or *minim* must acknowledge the God worshiped by Israel as the one true God. This requires confessing the truth that is in hand.

• Is the question of whether Jews and Christians believe in the same God categorically different from the question of whether Jews from different periods of time or radically different schools of thought believe in the same God? Yes, a continuity of conviction marks the state of the authentic monotheism in Israel over time. The Israelites from all periods have in common affirmed the unity of God and have told about themselves the established narratives of Scripture.

Does this question matter to them? We should have to establish as fact the diversity of conceptions of God that characterized Jews in different times and places. But what changed over time is the interpretation of the Scriptures of monotheism, not the principle. The paradox yields the last word: the *min* by his actions does recognize the God worshiped by Israel. His spite expressed in his misreading of Scripture is his act of faith, so he testifies to his faith by what he denies.

IV. The Perspective of Classical Judaism: The Status of the Idolaters, Who Are Subject to the Same Moral Authority as Israel

Thus far we have pursued the question of the status as to Israel of the *min,* not focusing on the idolater. The mode of portraying the *min* yielded a clear picture of his marginal status but his ultimate place in Israel. He knew the truth and denied it. What about the Gentiles? We now address the idolater. What places him outside the boundary of Israel altogether, while the *minim* belong on the borderline?

In a critical construction explaining the exclusion of the Gentiles and implicitly encompassing Israel, all humanity by its nature is subject to the Torah. The natural condition of humanity is violated by the Gentiles by reason of their indicative qualities. When the nations attain their natural condition, the condition in which God made them, they will become part of Israel. More exactly, they will revert to their natural and original character. As matters stand, the nations' distinctive qualities separate them from God. What is implicit in this proposition is that the natural condition of the Gentile assigns him a position alongside Israel in the presence of God. The unnatural condition of the Gentiles divides them up into particular nations and defines the difference between one Gentile and another. What is implicit will become clear when we have examined the monumental narratives that explain the human condition.

So now the question becomes urgent: How has this catastrophic differentiation imposed itself between Israel and the Gentiles, such that the Gentiles, for all their glory in the here and now, won for themselves the grave, while Israel, for all its humiliation in the present age, inherits the world to come? And the answer is self-evident from all that has been said: the Gentiles reject God, whom they could and should have known in the Torah. They rejected the Torah and all else followed. The proposition then moves in these simple steps:

1. Israel differs from the Gentiles because Israel possesses the Torah and the Gentiles do not;

2. the Gentiles rejected the Torah because it contradicts their nature; because of their character since they do not possess the Torah, the Gentiles worship idols instead of God; and

3. therefore God rejects the Gentiles and identifies with Israel.

Here monotheism intervenes: the conviction that the one God governs all humanity and does so justly. The status of the Gentiles testifies to the oneness of God: God's uniform justice in governing all of humanity. The oral Torah has to demonstrate the unity of God by showing that the same justice that governs Israel and endows Israel with the Torah dictates the fate of the Gentiles and denies them the Torah. And, predictably, that demonstration must further underscore the justice of the condition of the Gentiles: measure for measure must play itself out especially here.

The Gentiles are subject to the dominion of the one God but deprived themselves of the Torah because they rejected it, and, showing the precision of justice, the canonical sources hold they rejected the Torah because the Torah deprived them of the very practices or traits that they deemed characteristic, essential to their being. That circularity marks the tale of how things were to begin in fact describes how things always are; it is not historical but philosophical. The Gentiles' own character, the shape of their conscience, then, now, and always, accounts for their condition—which, by an act of will, they can change. What they did not want, that of which they were by their own word unworthy, is denied them. And what they do want condemns them. So when each nation comes under judgment for rejecting the Torah, the indictment of each is spoken out of its own mouth, its own self-indictment then forms the core of the matter.

When they protest the injustice of the decision that takes effect just then, they are shown the workings of the moral order, as the following quite systematic account of the governing pattern explains.

Bavli tractate Abodah Zarah 1:1 I.2/2a-b

    A. R. Hanina bar Pappa, and some say, R. Simlai, gave the following exposition [of the verse, "They that fashion a graven image are all of them vanity, and their delectable things shall not profit, and their own witnesses see not nor know" (Isa. 44:9)]: "In the age to come the Holy One, blessed be He, will bring a scroll of the Torah and hold it in his bosom and say, 'Let him who has kept himself busy with it come and take his reward.' Then all the gentiles will crowd together: 'All of the nations are gathered together' (Isa. 43:9). The Holy One, blessed be He, will say to them, 'Do not crowd together before me in a mob. But let each nation enter together with its scribes, 'and let the peoples be gathered together' (Isa. 43:9), and the word 'people' means 'kingdom': 'and one kingdom shall be stronger than the other' (Gen. 25:23)."

We note that the players are the principal participants in world history: the Romans first and foremost, then the Persians, the other world-rulers of the age:

C. "The kingdom of Rome comes in first."

H. "The Holy One, blessed be He, will say to them, 'How have you defined your chief occupation?'

I. "They will say before him, 'Lord of the world, a vast number of marketplaces have we set up, a vast number of bathhouses we have made, a vast amount of silver and gold have we accumulated. And all of these things we have done only in behalf of Israel, so that they may define as their chief occupation the study of the Torah.'

J. "The Holy One, blessed be He, will say to them, 'You complete idiots! Whatever you have done has been for your own convenience. You have set up a vast number of marketplaces to be sure, but that was so as to set up whorehouses in them. The bathhouses were for your own pleasure. Silver and gold belong to me anyhow: "Mine is the silver and mine is the gold, says the Lord of hosts" (Hag. 2:8). Are there any among you who have been telling of "this" and "this" is only the Torah: "And this is the Torah that Moses set before the children of Israel' (Deut. 4:44)." So they will make their exit, humiliated.

The claim of Rome—to support Israel in Torah-study—is rejected on grounds that the Romans did not exhibit the right attitude, always a dynamic force in the theology. Then the other world-ruler enters in with its claim:

K. "When the kingdom of Rome has made its exit, the kingdom of Persia enters afterward."

M. "The Holy One, blessed be He, will say to them, 'How have you defined your chief occupation?'

N. "They will say before him, 'Lord of the world, We have thrown up a vast number of bridges, we have conquered a vast number of towns, we have made a vast number of wars, and all of them we did only for Israel, so that they may define as their chief occupation the study of the Torah.'

O. "The Holy One, blessed be He, will say to them, 'Whatever you have done has been for your own convenience. You have thrown up a vast number of bridges, to collect tolls, you have conquered a vast number of towns, to collect the corvée, and, as to making a vast number of wars, I am the one who makes wars: "The Lord is a man of war" (Exod. 19:17). Are there any among you who have been telling of "this" and "this" is only the Torah: "And this is the Torah that Moses set before the children of Israel" (Deut. 4:44).' So they will make their exit, humiliated.

R. "And so it will go with each and every nation."

As native categories, Rome and Persia are singled out, "all the other nations" play no role, for reasons with which we are already familiar. Once more the theology reaches into its deepest thought on the power of intentionality, showing that what people want is what they get.

But matters cannot be limited to the two world empires of the present age, Rome and Iran, standing in judgment at the end of time. The theology values balance, proportion, seeks complementary relationships, and therefore treats beginnings along with endings, the one going over the ground of the other. Accordingly, a recapitulation of the same event—the Gentiles' rejection of the Torah—chooses as its setting not the last judgment but the first encounter, that is, the giving of the Torah itself. In the timeless world constructed by the oral Torah, what happens at the outset exemplifies how things always happen, and what happens at the end embodies what has always taken place. The basic thesis is identical—the Gentiles cannot accept the Torah because to do so they would have to deny their very character. But the exposition retains its interest because it takes its own course.

Now the Gentiles are not just Rome and Persia but others. Of special interest, the Torah is embodied in some of the Ten Commandments—not to murder, not to commit adultery, not to steal—so the Gentiles are rejected for not keeping the seven commandments assigned to the children of Noah. The upshot is that the reason that the Gentiles rejected the Torah is that the Torah prohibits deeds that the Gentiles do by their very nature. Israel ultimately is changed by the Torah, so Israel exhibits traits imparted by their encounter with the Torah. So, too, with the Gentiles. By their nature the Gentiles are what they are; the Torah has not changed their nature.

Once more a single standard applies to both components of humanity, but with opposite effect:

Sifré to Deuteronomy CCCXLIII: IV.1ff.

1. A. Another teaching concerning the phrase, "He said, 'The Lord came from Sinai'":

   B. When the Omnipresent appeared to give the Torah to Israel, it was not to Israel alone that he revealed himself but to every nation.

   C. First of all he came to the children of Esau. He said to them, "Will you accept the Torah?"

   D. They said to him, "What is written in it?"

   E. He said to them, "'You shall not murder' (Exod. 20:13)."

   F. They said to him, "The very being of 'those men' [namely, us] and of their father is to murder, for it is said, 'But the hands are the hands of Esau' (Gen. 27:22). 'By your sword you shall live' (Gen. 27:40)."

At this point we cover new ground: other classes of Gentiles that reject the Torah. Now the Torah's own narrative takes over, replacing the known facts of world politics, such as the earlier account sets forth, and instead supplying evidence out of Scripture as to the character of the Gentile group under discussion:

   G. So he went to the children of Ammon and Moab and said to them, "Will you accept the Torah?"

H. They said to him, "What is written in it?"

I. He said to them, "'You shall not commit adultery' (Exod. 20:13)."

J. They said to him, "The very essence of fornication belongs to them [us], for it is said, 'Thus were both the daughters of Lot with child by their fathers' (Gen. 19:36)."

K. So he went to the children of Ishmael and said to them, "Will you accept the Torah?"

L. They said to him, "What is written in it?"

M. He said to them, "'You shall not steal' (Exod. 20:13)."

N. They said to him, "The very essence of their [our] father is thievery, as it is said, 'And he shall be a wild ass of a man' (Gen. 16:12)."

O. And so it went. He went to every nation, asking them, "Will you accept the Torah?"

P. For so it is said, "All the kings of the earth shall give you thanks, O Lord, for they have heard the words of your mouth" (Ps. 138:4).

Q. Might one suppose that they listened and accepted the Torah?

R. Scripture says, "And I will execute vengeance in anger and fury upon the nations, because they did not listen" (Mic. 5:14).

At this point we turn back to the obligations that God has imposed upon the Gentiles; these obligations have no bearing upon the acceptance of the Torah; they form part of the ground of being, the condition of existence, of the Gentiles. Yet even here, the Gentiles do not accept God's authority in matters of natural law:

S. And it is not enough for them that they did not listen, but even the seven religious duties that the children of

39

Noah indeed accepted upon themselves they could not uphold before breaking them.

  T. When the Holy One, blessed be He, saw that that is how things were, he gave them to Israel.

Along these same lines, the Gentiles would like to make a common pact with Israel, but cannot have a share in God:

Sifré to Deuteronomy CCCXLIII: IX.2

  A. Thus the nations of the world would ask Israel, saying to them, "'What is your beloved more than another beloved' (Song 5:9)? For you are willing to accept death on his account."

  B. For so Scripture says, "Therefore they love you to death" (Song 1:3).

  C. And further: "No, but for your sake are we killed all day long" (Ps. 44:23).

Now comes the envy of the Gentiles, their desire to amalgamate with Israel, and Israel's insistence upon remaining a holy people, a people apart:

  D. [The nations continue,] "All of you are handsome, all of you are strong. Come and let us form a group in common."

  E. And the Israelites answer, "We shall report to you part of the praise that is coming to him, and in that way you will discern him:

  F. "'My beloved is white and ruddy . . . his head is as the most fine gold . . . his eyes are like doves beside the waterbrooks . . . his cheeks are as a bed of spices . . . his hands are as rods of gold . . . His legs are as pillars of marble . . . His mouth is most sweet, yes, he is altogether sweet'" (Song 5:10-16).

G. When the nations of the world hear about the beauty and praiseworthy quality of the Holy One, blessed be He, they say to them, "Let us come with you."

H. For it is said, "Where has your beloved gone, O you fairest among women? Where has your beloved turned, that we may seek him with you" (Song 5:1).

The various Gentile nations rejected the Torah for specific and reasonable considerations, concretely, because the Torah prohibited deeds essential to their being.

What then is the difference between the Gentile and the Israelite, individually and collectively? A picture in cartographic form of the theological anthropology of the oral Torah, would portray a many-colored Israel at the center of the circle, with the perimeter comprised by all-white Gentiles, since, in the *Halakhah,* Gentiles are a source of uncleanness of the same virulence as corpse-uncleanness; the perimeter would be an undifferentiated white, the color of death. The law of uncleanness bears its theological counterpart in the lore of death and resurrection, a single theology animating both. Gentile-idolaters and Israelite worshipers of the one and only God part company at death. Israelites die and rise from the grave, Gentiles die and remain there. The roads intersect at the grave, each component of humanity taking its own path beyond. Israelites—meaning, those possessed of right conviction—will rise from the grave, stand in judgment (along with some Gentiles, as we shall see in a moment), but then enter upon eternal life, to which no one else will enjoy access. So, in substance, humanity viewed whole is divided between those who get a share in the world to come—Israel—and who will stand when subject to divine judgment and those who will not.

If a Gentile keeps the Torah, he is saved. But by keeping the Torah, the Gentile has ceased to be Gentile and becomes Israelite, worthy even of the high priesthood. First comes the definition of how Israel becomes Israel, which is by accepting God's dominion in the Torah:

Sifra CXCIV: ii.1

1. A. "The Lord spoke to Moses saying, Speak to the Israelite people and say to them, I am the Lord your God":

   B. R. Simeon b. Yohai says, "That is in line with what is said elsewhere: 'I am the Lord your God [who brought you out of the land of Egypt, out of the house of bondage]' (Exod. 20:2).

   C. "'Am I the Lord, whose sovereignty you took upon yourself in Egypt?'

   D. "They said to him, 'Indeed.'

   E. "'Indeed you have accepted my dominion.'

   F. "'They accepted my decrees: "You will have no other gods before me."'

   G. "That is what is said here: 'I am the Lord your God,' meaning, 'Am I the one whose dominion you accepted at Sinai?'

   H. "They said to him, 'Indeed.'

   I. "'Indeed you have accepted my dominion.'

   J. "They accepted my decrees: 'You shall not copy the practices of the land of Egypt where you dwelt, or of the land of Canaan to which I am taking you; nor shall you follow their laws.'"

I cite the passage to underscore how matters are defined, which is by appeal to the Torah. Then the true state of affairs emerges when the same definition explicitly is brought to bear upon the Gentiles. That yields the clear inference that Gentiles have the power to join themselves to Israel as fully-naturalized Israelites, so the Torah that defines their status also constitutes the ticket of admission to the world to come that Israel will enter in due course. Sages could not be more explicit than they are when they insist that the Gentile ceases to be in the status of the Gentile when he accepts God's rule in the Torah:

Sifra CXCIV: ii.15

15. A. "... by the pursuit of which man shall live":

   B. R. Jeremiah says, "How do I know that even a gentile who keeps the Torah, lo, he is like the high priest?

   C. "Scripture says, 'by the pursuit of which man shall live.'"

   D. And so he says, "'And this is the Torah of the priests, Levites, and Israelites,' is not what is said here, but rather, 'This is the Torah of the man, O Lord God' (2 Sam. 7:19)."

   E. And so he says, "'Open the gates and let priests, Levites, and Israelites will enter it' is not what is said, but rather, 'Open the gates and let the righteous nation, who keeps faith, enter it' (Isa. 26:2)."

   F. And so he says, "'This is the gate of the Lord. Priests, Levites, and Israelites. . .' is not what is said, but rather, 'the righteous shall enter into it' (Ps. 118:20)."

   G. And so he says, "'What is said is not, 'Rejoice, priests, Levites, and Israelites,' but rather, 'Rejoice, O righteous, in the Lord' (Ps. 33:1)."

   H. And so he says, "It is not, 'Do good, O Lord, to the priests, Levites, and Israelites,' but rather, 'Do good, O Lord, to the good, to the upright in heart' (Ps. 125:4)."

   I. "Thus, even a gentile who keeps the Torah, lo, he is like the high priest."

That is not to suggest God does not rule the Gentiles. He does—whether they like it or not, acknowledge him or not. God responds also to the acts of merit taken by Gentiles, as much as to those of Israel. The upshot is, "Gentile" and "Israel" classify through the presence or absence of the same traits; they form taxonomic categories that can, in the case of the Gentile, change when that which is classified requires reclassification.

Tosefta-tractate Abodah Zarah 8:4-6

A. Concerning religious requirements were the children of Noah admonished:

B. setting up courts of justice, idolatry, blasphemy [cursing the Name of God], fornication, bloodshed, and thievery.

We now proceed to show how each of these religious obligations is represented as applying to Gentiles as much as to Israelites:

C. Concerning setting up courts of justice—how so [how does Scripture or reason validate the claim thatGentiles are to set up courts of justice]?

D. Just as Israelites are commanded to call into session in their towns courts of justice.

E. Concerning idolatry and blasphemy—how so? . . .

F. Concerning fornication—how so?

G. "On account of any form of prohibited sexual relationship on account of which an Israelite court inflicts the death-penalty, the children of Noah are subject to warning," the words of R. Meir.

H. And sages say, "There are many prohibited relationships, on account of which an Israelite court does not inflict the death-penalty and the children of Noah are [not] warned. In regard to these forbidden relationships the nations are judged in accord with the laws governing the nations.

I. "And you have only the prohibitions of sexual relations with a betrothed maiden alone."

The systemization of Scripture's evidence for the stated proposition continues:

8:5 A. For bloodshed—how so?

B. A gentile [who kills] a gentile and a gentile who kills an Israelite are liable. An Israelite [who kills] a gentile is exempt.

C. Concerning thievery?

D. [If] one has stolen, or robbed, and so too in the case of finding a beautiful captive [woman], and in similar cases:

E. a gentile in regard to a gentile, or a gentile in regard to an Israelite—it is prohibited. And an Israelite in regard to a gentile—it is permitted.

8:6 A. Concerning a limb cut from a living beast—how so?

B. A dangling limb on a beast, [which] is not [so connected] as to bring about healing,

C. is forbidden for use by the children of Noah, and, it goes without saying, for Israelites.

D. But if there is [in the connecting flesh] sufficient [blood supply] to bring about healing,

E. it is permitted to Israelites, and, it goes without saying, to the children of Noah.

Nothing intrinsic distinguishes Israel from the Gentiles, only their attitudes and actions. Opinion coalesces around the proposition that Israel and the Gentiles do form a single genus, speciated by the relationship to God and the Torah. So in the end, a ferocious Israelite or a forbearing Gentile represent mere anomalies, not categorical imperatives. Sufficient proof derives from the explicit statement that when Israel acts like Gentiles, it enters the classification of Gentiles; if Israel conducts itself like the Gentiles, Israel will be rejected and punished as were the Gentiles, with special reference to Egypt and Canaan. This matter is spelled out in another formally perfect composition:

Sifra CXCIII: I.1-11

1. B. "The Lord spoke to Moses saying, Speak to the Israelite people and say to them, I am the Lord your God":

C. "I am the Lord," for I spoke and the world came into being.

45

D. "I am full of mercy."

E. "I am Judge to exact punishment and faithful to pay recompense."

F. "I am the one who exacted punishment from the generation of the Flood and the men of Sodom and Egypt, and I shall exact punishment from you if you act like them."

First comes Egypt:

2. A. And how do we know that there was never any nation among all of the nations that practiced such abominations, more than did the Egyptians?

B. Scripture says, "You shall not copy the practices of the land of Egypt where you dwelt."

C. And how do we know that the last generation did more abhorrent things than all the rest of them?

D. Scripture says, "You shall not copy the practices of the land of Egypt."

E. And how do we know that the people in the last location in which the Israelites dwelt were more abhorrent than all the rest?

F. Scripture says, ". . . where you dwelt, you shall not do."

G. And how do we know that the fact that the Israelites dwelt there was the cause for all these deeds?

H. Scripture says, "You shall not copy . . . where you dwelt."

Now we deal with the Canaanites, following the given form:

3. A. How do we know that there was never a nation among all the nations that did more abhorrent things than the Canaanites?

B. Scripture says, "You shall not copy the practices . . . of the land of Canaan [to which I am taking you; nor shall you follow their laws]."

C. And how do we know that the last generation did more abhorrent things than all the rest of them?

D. Scripture says, "You shall not copy the practices of the land of Canaan."

E. And how do we know that the people in the place to which the Israelites were coming for conquest were more abhorrent than all the rest?

F. Scripture says, ". . . to which I am taking you."

G. And how do we know that it is the arrival of the Israelites that caused them to do all these deeds?

H. Scripture says, "or of the land of Canaan to which I am taking you; nor shall you follow their laws."

Now the two cases are expounded in the same terms, and the specific type of laws that Israel is not to follow is defined:

7. A. If "You shall not copy the practices of the land of Egypt . . . or of the land of Canaan,"

B. might one think that they are not to build their buildings or plant vineyards as they did?

C. Scripture says, "nor shall you follow their laws":

D. "I have referred only to the rules that were made for them and for their fathers and their fathers' fathers."

E. And what would they do?

F. A man would marry a man, and a woman would marry a woman, a man would marry a woman and her daughter, a woman would be married to two men.

G. That is why it is said, "nor shall you follow their laws."

8. A. ["My rules alone shall you observe and faithfully follow my laws":]

B. "my rules": this refers to laws.

C. ". . . my laws": this refers to the amplifications thereof.

D. ". . . shall you observe": this refers to repeating traditions.

E. ". . . and faithfully follow": this refers to concrete deed.

F. ". . . and faithfully follow my laws": it is not the repetition of traditions that is the important thing but doing them is the important thing.

At stake in differentiating Israel from the Gentiles is life in the world to come; the Gentiles offer only death:

9. A. "You shall keep my laws and my rules, by the pursuit of which man [shall live]":

B. This formulation of matter serves to make keeping and doing into laws, and keeping and doing into rules.

10. A. ". . . shall live":

B. in the world to come.

C. And should you wish to claim that the reference is to this world, is it not the fact that in the end one dies?

D. Lo, how am I to explain, ". . . shall live"?

E. It is with reference to the world to come.

11. A. "I the Lord am your God":

B. faithful to pay a reward.

Here we find the entire doctrine of the Gentiles fully exposed. God judges Israel and the Gentiles by a single rule of justice; to each is meted out measure for measure. Israel is not elect by reason of privilege; Israel is elect solely because Israel accepts the Torah and so knows God. The same punishment exacted from the generation of the Flood, the Sodomites, the Egyptians, and all others will be exacted from Israel if Israel acts like them. At that point, Israel becomes Gentile. It is the Torah that differentiates.

The attitude of the idolater governs God's disposition of matters. God hates idolaters more than he hates the idol itself, for, all parties concur, in any case there is no substance in idolatry itself. The idolater rejects God and so makes the idol. So what is at issue in idolatry is the attitude of the idolater, that is, his rejection of the one true God, made manifest in the Torah. The idolater by his attitude and intention confers upon the idol a status that on its own the idol cannot attain, being inanimate in any event. So the logic that governs distinguishes the actor from the acted upon, the cause from that which is caused, and the rest follows.

Now the Gentiles are not just Rome and Persia but others; and of special interest, the Torah is embodied in some of the Ten Commandments—not to murder, not to commit adultery, not to steal; then the Gentiles are rejected for not keeping the seven commandments assigned to the children of Noah. The upshot is that the reason that the Gentiles rejected the Torah is that the Torah prohibits deeds that the Gentiles do by their very nature. Israel ultimately is changed by the Torah so that Israel exhibits traits imparted by their encounter with the Torah. So, too, with the Gentiles, by their nature they are what they are; the Torah has not changed their nature.

Once more a single standard applies to both components of humanity, but with opposite effect:

Sifré to Deuteronomy CCCXLIII:IV.1ff.:

1. A. Another teaching concerning the phrase, "He said, 'The Lord came from Sinai'":

   B. When the Omnipresent appeared to give the Torah to Israel, it was not to Israel alone that he revealed himself but to every nation.

   C. First of all he came to the children of Esau. He said to them, "Will you accept the Torah?"

   D. They said to him, "What is written in it?"

   E. He said to them, "'You shall not murder' (Exod. 20:13)."

   F. They said to him, "The very being of 'those men' [namely, us] and of their father is to murder, for it is said, 'But

49

the hands are the hands of Esau' (Gen. 27:22). 'By your sword you shall live' (Gen. 27:40)."

At this point we cover new ground: other classes of Gentiles that reject the Torah; now the Torah's own narrative takes over, replacing the known facts of world politics, such as the earlier account sets forth, and instead supplying evidence out of Scripture as to the character of the Gentile group under discussion:

G. So he went to the children of Ammon and Moab and said to them, "Will you accept the Torah?"

H. They said to him, "What is written in it?"

I. He said to them, "'You shall not commit adultery' (Exod. 20:13)."

J. They said to him, "The very essence of fornication belongs to them [us], for it is said, 'Thus were both the daughters of Lot with child by their fathers' (Gen. 19:36)."

K. So he went to the children of Ishmael and said to them, "Will you accept the Torah?"

L. They said to him, "What is written in it?"

M. He said to them, "'You shall not steal' (Exod. 20:13)."

N. They said to him, "The very essence of their [our] father is thievery, as it is said, 'And he shall be a wild ass of a man' (Gen. 16:12)."

O. And so it went. He went to every nation, asking them, "Will you accept the Torah?"

P. For so it is said, "All the kings of the earth shall give you thanks, O Lord, for they have heard the words of your mouth" (Ps. 138:4).

Q. Might one suppose that they listened and accepted the Torah?

R. Scripture says, "And I will execute vengeance in anger and fury upon the nations, because they did not listen" (Mic. 5:14).

At this point we turn back to the obligations that God has imposed upon the Gentiles; these obligations have no bearing upon the acceptance of the Torah; they form part of the ground of being, the condition of existence, of the Gentiles. Yet even here, the Gentiles do not accept God's authority in matters of natural law:

S. And it is not enough for them that they did not listen, but even the seven religious duties that the children of Noah indeed accepted upon themselves they could not uphold before breaking them.

T. When the Holy One, blessed be He, saw that that is how things were, he gave them to Israel.

Humanity divides into Israel with the Torah, and the Gentiles with their idols. The one is destined to life eternal with God, the other to the grave, there to spend eternity. World order then finds its center and focus in Israel, and whatever happens that counts under Heaven's gaze takes place in relationship to Israel. That division yields rich and dense details but only a simple story, easily retold. In a purposeful act of benevolence, the just God created the world in so orderly a way that the principle of justice and equity governs throughout. Fair rules apply equally to all persons and govern under all circumstances. God not only created man but made himself known to man through the Torah. But man, possessed of free will, enjoys the choice of accepting and obeying the Torah, therefore living in the kingdom of heaven, or rejecting the Torah and God in favor of idolatry and idols.

Now we realize the full potentiality contained in the simple doctrines with which we began: those who accept the Torah are called Israel, and the others are called Gentiles. The Gentiles hate Israel because of the Torah, and they also hate God. But the world as now constituted is such that the Gentiles rule, and Israel is subjugated. Where is the

51

justice in that inversion of right, with God's people handed over to the charge of God's enemies? Israel has sinned, so rebelled against God, and the Gentiles then form God's instrument for the punishment of Israel. God's justice governs, the world conforms to orderly rules, embedded in the very structure of creation. Israel's own condition stands as the surest testimony of the world's good and just order. That guarantee is for now and all time to come.

V. Concluding Contemporary Postscript

The classical and normative sources of law and theology have guided us into a cul-de-sac. Judaic monotheism expounded by its normative sources cannot acknowledge the claim to truth of any other monotheism, even though all monotheisms concur on the same theological logic. Christianity and Islam concur on the unity of God and can recite the Shema, "Hear Israel the Lord our God the Lord is one," except for the opening invocation. Surely if you and I concur on the same proposition about God, that he is one—just and merciful, omnipotent and unique—we should be able to recognize our agreement. When we say that God is one and unique, we aver that there can be no other being like God in uniqueness. It must follow that all who affirm the unity and uniqueness of God speak of the same God.

Yet when we survey the classical and normative sources of Judaism we produce the contradiction: Judaism declares God to be one but denies the comparable declaration of Christianity and Islam that God is uniquely one. Is the monotheism of Judaism in its classical statement different in its characteristics from the monotheism of Christianity or Islam? The answer is, only if there are variations to the definition of monotheism. But while polytheism makes provision for diversity, monotheism does not. The very logic of monotheism governs and defines the outcome: all religious systems that affirm the unity of God necessarily speak of one and the same God.

The position of Judaism cannot defy logic and must give way to its requirements. Monotheism stands in judgment upon all monotheist systems. Contemporary Judaism parts company from the received system in submitting to the judgment of monotheist logic: there can be and there is only one God, and all who affirm one God affirm that one and the same God. That is so even though all who recognize many gods do not by definition affirm the same god. The dialogue among Judaism, Christianity, and Islam begins with the criticism of the purity of the monotheism affirmed by the competing monotheist systems.

Interfaith dialogue is made possible by monotheism, which defines the common ground on the foundations of which debate can take place. Polytheism defines dialogue out of existence, making provision, rather, for an exchange of opinions in a spirit of tolerance. Since the polytheist religions lay no claim to unique possession of the truth, nothing is left about which to contend. That is why Judaism stands in judgment of Christianity and Islam specifically as these form explications of the meaning of the unity and uniqueness of God, and Judaism—so Judaism must claim—sets the standard for true monotheism. Christianity and Islam claim the same right of judgment of the competition. The anomaly of the classical statement of Judaism—that only Judaism affirms authentic monotheism—yields the only true interfaith dialogue. That is defined as a debate on the same issues resting on the same premises.

Chapter 3

....

One God, the Same God?

Bruce D. Chilton

Introduction

Belief that God is one carries immediate implications. It means that a single source stands behind the creation of the heavens and the earth, so all forms of reality share a foundation in the divine; it means that suffering, as well as blessing proceed from God; it means that the transcendence of God is accessible to human faith.

To assert God's sameness in the three Abrahamic religions may seem straightforward, following from God's oneness; some version of that claim is often heard. But exclusions of faith perspectives, both across theologies and within theological traditions, are considerable when the Abrahamic religions are privileged with this assumption.

Across theologies, if God is the same in Christianity, Islam, and Judaism, does that imply that conceptions of the divine in Hinduism and Buddhism, for example, differ constitutionally from Abrahamic conceptions? Might the assertion of sameness reinforce a view of God in which "Abraham" alone shows humanity how to believe? If the issue is approached from the point of view of monotheism, that raises the attendant questions of whether and when a religion is indeed monotheist, and why—for example, Gnosticism, Sikhism, and Zoroastrianism are not included.

Then, within theological traditions, how might "sameness" be construed, when the historical fact of division, often over conceptions of God, features persistently in the histories of Christianity, Islam, and Judaism? To mention some medieval disagreements with continuing impact, did Martin Luther and Pope Leo, or Ibn Sina and al-Ghazali, or Ben Maimon and Ben Nachman believe in the "same" God?

Despite these complexities, the three Abrahamic traditions assert their faith in what they describe as one God in documents they hold as classic or canonical. In addition to the recognized Scriptures of each (Tanakh, the Old and New Testaments, the Qur'an), the interpretative perspectives of Rabbinic, Patristic, and Hadith literatures set out standards of coherent discourse as well as authoritative findings. Within that discourse, cogent and comparable views of the one God are set out.

Classic sources of Christianity developed theories of how God as revealed to historic Israel relates to God as revealed in Christ. This issue directly addresses how Judaism and Christianity can be conceived in their continuity and in their difference. But the way early Christian thinkers posed the question enabled them to speak across a spectrum of religions and philosophies: they addressed any system of thought that focuses on how "reason" (*logos*) governs the world. Justin Martyr articulated the theology of Christ as the *logos*, already embedded in the Gospel according to John, in a way that has proven influential (Part I). Early Christian views of God's Spirit (Part II) provide a basis on which contrasts may be drawn with other religions that are anchored in revelation, even those such as Islam that are articulated after the period in which classic Christian sources were composed. By considering the twin concerns of God as Creator and God as Revealer, our conclusion will suggest that believing in one God dedicates theology to comparison, but does not necessitate the claim of the same God.

Part I: Jesus and *Logos*

The fourth Gospel develops a distinctive vocabulary in order to articulate Jesus' impact upon humanity, which is largely derived from the theological language of the Targumim, the Aramaic paraphrases of the Hebrew Bible employed within worship in synagogues. Jesus is explained in terms of God's "word," *logos* in Greek, *memra* in Aramaic. *Memra*, a nominal form of the verb "to speak" (*amar*), is the Targumic reference to God's activity of commanding. God might simply be thought of as commanding what is ordered when the term is used, but the emphasis might also fall on how people respond to the order or on what lies behind the divine order and the human response. *Memra* might convey a range of emphases, both interior to the act of commanding, informing the decision of command, and consequent upon the act, devolving from it. Context alone permits us to make a selection among its various senses. There is no such thing as a single *concept* of God's *memra*, certainly not as personal being or hypostasis, nor even a systematic idea that is fully consistent from Targum to Targum. What links the Targumim, in their distinct usages of *memra*, is not a theological thought, but a theological manner of speaking of God in terms of divine commanding. *Memra* is not invoked haphazardly when some verb of speaking happens to be used of God in the Hebrew text that is rendered. The Targums suggest that the usage of the term reflects the ways in which given interpreters conceived of God's intention in the command or the human response to what is effected by the command.

The prologue of John's Gospel presents a particular construal of how Jesus Christ personally might be understood as a part of God's commanding *logos* or *memra*.[1] The first usage of *logos* in the Gospel simply establishes its identity with God (and not—it must be emphasized—with Jesus, 1:1[2]):

"In the beginning was the word, and the word was related to God, and the word was God."

The word is identified as the creative, primordial source of what exists (1:2, 3), in a way quite consistent with the association of *memra* and creation within the Targumim.

The common notion that the *logos* is to be identified immediately with Jesus in the prologue is to some extent based upon a reading of the text in Greek which does not attend adequately to its obviously deliberate sequence. God's *logos* is said to be the place where "life" is, and that life is held to be the "light" of all humanity (v. 4). Insofar as an immediately Christological category is developed in the prologue, that category is "light," not "word." It is the "light" which shines in the darkness (v. 5), which enlightens every person (v. 9). Most crucially, the "light," a neuter noun in Greek (*to phos*), is identified as masculine and singular in verse 10:

"In it was the world, and the world came into existence through it, and the world did not know *him.*"

From that textual moment, the usage of pronouns and the summary reference to Jesus' ministry (vv. 11-13, cf. vv. 6-8) makes it clear we are dealing with a person, not an entity. But the telling factor is that Jesus has been presented, precisely and grammatically, as the light that takes its origin in the *logos,* rather than as the *logos* in itself.

We then come to the clause that has dominated the reading of the fourth Gospel, and which has served as a cornerstone of a Christological construction of the *logos* in Christian theology from the second century (v. 14a):

"And the *logos* became flesh and dwelt among us."

Once *logos* has been identified with Jesus, as it is for Clement of Alexandria and Irenaeus during the second century, the reference of the clause can only be to the Incarnation. Indeed, the Latin text of the clause, *et verbum caro factum est,* is conventionally taken in association with the creedal assertion that the "Son," understood as the second person of the Trinity, became incarnate (*incarnatus est*). But all such readings and construals are possible only on the assumption that the *logos* and Jesus are interchangeable; then he is a preexistent, personal entity come down from heaven. The problem with such an exegesis of the Johannine text is the care with which Jesus is *not* directly associated with the *logos* in verses 1-13.

But if verse 14 is not read as asserting a Christological Incarnation, what else can it be saying? An approach to that question which is guided by our observation of the usage of *memra* in the Targumim suggests an answer. *Memra* is essentially God's mighty command, vindicating and warning his people; verse 14 refers to this *logos* as becoming flesh and then explains that assertion by saying it "dwelt among us," (*eskenosen en hemin*). The verb *skenoo*, it is often observed, relates naturally to *shakhen* in Hebrew and Aramaic, from which *Shekhinah*, the principal term of reference to God's presence in the cult, is derived. To describe the *logos*, understood as *memra*, as dwelling among us such that we might behold its glory, is consistent with Targumic usage.

The "glory" beheld is subjected to a precise qualification at the end of the verse; it is "glory as of an only one with a Father, full of grace and truth" (1:14c). The assertion is *not* "we have beheld his glory, glory as of the only Son from the Father," as in the Revised Standard Version; still less is it, "we have seen his glory, the glory of the one and only Son, who came from the Father," as in the New International Version. The definite articles are conspicuously absent from the text in Greek; the glory spoken of is as of *an* only child, not "the only Son." The comparison is straightforwardly metaphorical, not doctrinal: the glory of *logos* was as a child's, reflecting the Father's.

Now, however, comes the element of genuine complexity in the logic of the Greek text: the glory of the *logos* is "as of an only one (*hos monogenous*) with a Father," and we know, as readers of the Gospel, that Jesus is God's Son. Indeed, we know explicitly from the body of the Gospel that Jesus, as God's "Son," speaks God's "word,"[3] and that the reaction to the one is congruent with the reaction to the other. The inference that the glory of the *logos* was "as of" Jesus is precisely consonant with the presentation of the Gospel as a whole. Jesus speaks the word of God; as the Son who was sent by his Father, he permits God's own voice to be heard.

The remainder of the prologue reflects the maintenance of the distinction between the *logos* and Jesus and suggests the sense in which we should understand that the *logos* "became flesh." John, we are told, witnessed "concerning it" (*peri autou*, that is, the word), by saying of Jesus,

"This was he of whom I said, He who comes after me . . ." (v. 15).

Fundamentally, the *logos* is still more the object of the prologue's attention than Jesus himself is, and that continues to be the case in verse 16:

"For from the fullness [*autou*] we have all received, even grace upon grace."

Autou, whether taken of the *logos* or of Jesus, is a masculine pronoun, but the statement is a resumption of what has been said in verses 3-5: we live from devolutions of the *logos*, the dynamic structure of word, light and life.

The understanding that God's "word" is still the essential issue in play makes the transition to the next topic straightforward (v. 17):

"For the law was given through Moses, grace and truth came through Jesus Christ."

The connection of *logos*, taken as *memra*, to the revelation through Moses is evident. Moreover, the syntax and logic of verse 17 coheres with that of verse 16; the coordination of God's activity in creation with his donation of the law through Moses is established within Targumic usage.

The link between the verses is literal, as well. The "grace" (*he kharis*) that came through Jesus Christ (v. 17) is correlative to the "grace upon grace" (*kharin anti kharitos*) we have all received (v. 16). There is a constant and consistent activity of God's *logos* from the creation and through the revelations to Moses and to Jesus. The *logos* in John develops well-established notions of the *memra* in early Judaism. At no point and in no way does the prologue present the revelation through Jesus as disjunctive with the revelation through Moses: any such disjunction is an artifact of imposing an anachronistic Christology upon the text. Verse 17 also provides guidance in regard to the reading of verse 14. The statement that grace and truth "came" (*egeneto*) through Jesus Christ is comparable to the assertion that God's word "became" (*egeneto*) flesh; in both cases, the underlying contention is that Jesus is the person in whom God's "word," His activity in creating and revealing, is manifest.

The last verse of the prologue is also the last word of the present reading. Verse 18 makes an assertion which makes any exclusively incarnational reading appear nonsensical:

"No one has at any time seen God; an only begotten, God, who was in the bosom of the Father, that one has made him known."

The first clause makes no sense whatever if the prologue means to say that Jesus simply is the *logos*. If the *logos* is God (v. 1:1), and Jesus is that "word," verse 18 is more than paradoxical. But verse 18 makes eminent sense on just the reading we have here suggested: no one has at any time seen God, provided the reader has followed the logic of his revelation as the prologue outlines it. Jesus, as an only begotten (again, without the article) has made God known (*exegesato*). Jesus is the word made flesh in the fourth Gospel, not the word *simpliciter*. Just as we would expect on the basis of our reading of passages that refer to *logos* in the body of the Gospel, Jesus is presented as the exegesis of God, the one who speaks his word. In that role, the fourth Gospel can refer to Jesus as God (*theos*) just as Philo refers to Moses[4]: not to make an ontological assertion, but to insist that the instrument of God's word is to be taken as divinely valued.

In a similar way, Justin Martyr during the second century believed that the apostles preach the *Logos* of God (*Dialogue* 109), and that is also what Paul and Barnabas say they articulate (Acts 13:46) after the synagogue leaders invite them to speak of *logos parakleseos* (13:15). God's *Logos* is so closely tied to prophecy for Justin, Balaam's oracle—the scriptural justification for the Bar Kokhba revolt—is attributed to Moses (*Dialogue* 106.4; 126.1). Eric Osborn has observed the role of the *Logos* in prophecy of all types in Justin: "Prophecy is the word of the logos and not merely a part of the logos."[5]

The fit is so tight that Osborn claims that Justin sometimes does not distinguish the *Logos* from the prophetic Spirit. In discussing the appearance at Mamre, Justin invokes what the "Word" says, or the "holy prophetic Spirit" (*Dialogue* 56). The connection of the *Logos* with inspiration become explicit when Justin says *Apology* 36:1:

> When you hear the utterances (*lexeis*) of the prophets spoken as by a player, don't think that they were spoken by those inspired, but think rather by the divine *Logos* who moved them.

His picture of the *Logos* is indeed dynamic, and the distinction between the *Logos* and the Spirit needs sorting out. Appreciating Justin's context, both Judaic and Hellenistic, permits a resolution of the question.

Philo's *Logos*, together with its Stoic and Platonic resonances and its relationship to Justin, has long been a part of discussion, and generally this ground has been better covered than most aspects of the study of Justin.[6] The closer the association with Socrates (*Apology* 46.3), and the more universal the claim of the reach of the *Logos* "in which the whole human race partakes" (*Apology* 46.2), the more natural this seems. Philo's case, argued in his brilliant continuous commentary on the Pentateuch in Greek, identified the creative *logos* behind our world and in our minds as the Torah that God revealed perfectly to Moses. Justin, in a less voluminous way, more the essayist than the systematician, insisted that our knowledge of the *Logos* implies that it is eternally human (cf. *Dialogue* 62). More specifically, he calibrated his case to address the reason (*logos*) that should animate imperial policy (*Apology* 2:1)[7]:

> Reason (*Logos*) enjoins those who are truly reverent and philosophers to honor and desire only the true . . .

Yet it is striking that Justin says that *both Jews and* Christians agree that "those who prophesy are God-born by nothing other than divine

Logos" (*Apology* 33.9). He even has Trypho say the *Logos* speaks in Scripture (Dialogue 68.5). Something of the qualities of Justin's conception should, therefore, be discernible in Judaic sources apart from Philo.

Oskar Skarsaune has suggested that biblical works such as Proverbs (to which Justin refers in *Dialogue* 61) and pseudipigraphal references such as 4 Maccabees 5:22-25 should be taken into account.[8] If we pursue this line of inquiry, the fit between prophecy and "word" in the Judaism of Justin's period, we are brought to *Targum Jonathan to the Prophets* and its usage of the term *Memra*. This term has in the past been explored in relation to John's Gospel, as has been mentioned,[9] but it may even more fruitfully be investigated in relation to second-century literature. The *Memra* is portrayed in the Targumim as active at the beginning of creation, as being directed in the mouths of the prophets by the Holy Spirit, and as being subject to rejection as well as acceptance by the people of God, among other usages. As a result, as the *Logos* in *Dialogue* 141, the *Memra* may speak of punishment as well as blessing. In the Targumim, as in Justin, the *memra/Logos* is the act of speaking, while Spirit of Prophecy/prophetic Spirit is the power of speech. Justin can be bold in his application of the possibilities these usages offer precisely because they are so widely agreed as to be axiomatic. Even the old man who Justin said explained the significance of Christ to him, like the Prophets, speaks the "divine word," *theion logon* (*Dialogue* 23.3).[10]

After the old man left Justin, a fire suddenly kindled in his soul, and he found the one sure and useful philosophy, which we have come to call Christianity (*Dialogue* 8.1). Bobichon observes the Platonic connection with fire,[11] but that is another case of a very widely appearing image, specifically connected in Luke 24:32 to the moment when the risen Jesus "opened" the Scriptures to two of his disciples. Justin also compares fire to how, when we say something, "we engender a word," but without any diminution or loss to ourselves (*Dialogue* 61.2).

With knowing innovation, Justin appropriates the Prophetic Spirit and *Logos* to Christianity. And he uses this appropriation to articulate a consistent Eucharistic theology (*Apology* 66.2):

> Because we do not take as ordinary bread or ordinary drink, but in the same way as through God's Logos Jesus Christ our incarnate savior had flesh and blood for our salvation, so also the food given thanks for through an oath of a Logos from him, from which our blood and flesh are nourished by assimilation, is—we have learned—the flesh and blood of that incarnate Jesus.

In this case Justin builds upon the Johannine understanding of Eucharist, as consumption of Jesus, which can only have offended Jewish readers and hearers.[12] To a dramatic extent, Justin locates himself within this conscious separation from Judaism, at the same time that he perfects his synthetic understanding of the *Logos*.

How specifically aware Justin was of Jewish teaching, specifically in its Rabbinic form, remains unclear. Yet anyone who is familiar with the development of Judaism from the second century onward will appreciate the irony of his understanding of Judaic interpretation. The second century was just the period when Scripture was being interpreted within Judaism in terms of its eternal meaning, when any limitation to its immediate reference came to be overridden by an appeal to the significance of the eternal Torah.

Both Judaism and Christianity made the immediate reference of Scripture ancillary to its systemic significance. But because Christianity was committed to the *Logos* as its systemic center, and Judaism to the Torah as its systemic center, the two could not understand one another. Any objection from one side to the other seems to miss the systemic point. In the absence of a language to discuss systemic relationship, the two sides fell to disputing which made better sense of the immediate reference (the "literal meaning," as would be said today) of the texts concerned.

The ground Justin chooses to fight on is redolent of his social location. His argument is not likely to have convinced a Jew like Trypho. In his *Dialogue with Trypho*, Justin portrays Trypho as being limited to the immediate reference of Scripture, enslaved by its specification of laws. Justin is committed to a typological reading of Scripture, the Christian norm during the second century. The prophets were understood to represent "types" of Christ, impressions on their minds of the heavenly reality, God's own son. Trypho, by contrast, is portrayed as becoming lost in the immediate minutiae of the prophetic text. So prevalent was this understanding of Judaism, by the end of the century, Christians such as Clement of Alexandria and Tertullian called any limitation to the immediate reference of Scripture (its "literal meaning") the "Jewish sense."

Justin presents the shift in the possession of the Spirit that animates the Scripture, moreover, in a way Paul does not. While Paul famously still hopes that "all Israel will be saved" (Rom. 11:26), Justin is categorical—by means of Isaiah 51:4 and Jeremiah 31:31—that "there is to be an ultimate Law and Covenant superior to all, which now must be kept by all people who claim God's inheritance" (*Dialogue* 11.2–3). This eternal covenant (Isa. 55:3-4) establishes who is a true, spiritual Israelite *and* Judaite, and who is not (*Dialogue* 11.5), taking the place of all other aspirants to those names.

Yet perhaps the true target of Justin's argument is not "Trypho" at all, but—as Graham Stanton has suggested[13]—his friends. Those styled "believing Pharisees" in Acts 15:5 insisted upon the covenant of circumcision in any assertion of faith in Christ, and there is good evidence that position thrived through and beyond the second century.[14] If that is the case, it would be one of example of how Justin's arguments might be related to the evolving social history of the second century.

Looking back, from a distance of several centuries, at a position that Justin articulated, Tanchuma (Y. Titissa 34) observed:

> Moses wanted to write Mishnah, as well [as the Torah]. But the Holy One, Blessed be He, foresaw that ultimately the

nations of the world translate the Torah into Greek and would claim, "We are Israel."

At the moment, we cannot prove that the Rabbis read Justin, any more than that Justin read the Rabbis. But the Rabbis interpreted him correctly, with or without direct knowledge of his works, because they understood that Christians claimed that they were Israel and that the instrument of their claim was the Prophetic corpus.

Part II. Spirit and Baptism

At the level of theology and at the level of practice, the development of the movement Jesus began into Christianity is punctuated by two drastic changes. The first change is when Jesus himself stopped baptizing people after the example of John the Baptist, his own rabbi (see John 3:22). The second change is proportionate to and symmetrical with the first: after Jesus was experienced as risen from the dead, his disciples began to immerse people in water in dedication to him (as they said in Greek, "into the name of Jesus"). Baptism in that sense became a paradigmatic ritual within Christianity.

In a study of baptism in the New Testament, Lars Hartman has observed that the phrase "into the name of" is not idiomatic Greek, but more probably reflects the Aramaic *leshun* (or Hebrew *leshem*). He adduces a passage from the Mishnah (Zebahim 4:6) in order to explain the meaning of the phrase.[15] There, the phrase clearly refers to those "for the sake of" whom a given sacrifice is offered.[16] Having understood that the generative meaning of the phrase is cultic, Hartman explains the significance of baptism in terms of the new community that is called into being:

> Here the people of the new covenant were gathered, cleansed, forgiven, sanctified, and equipped with a new spirit. Indeed, the gathering itself can also be regarded as occurring "into the name of the Lord Jesus."[17]

Such an emphasis on the role of God's Spirit in baptism is fundamental from the point of view of the New Testament itself. Whether the formulation is of immersion "into" or "in" Jesus' name, the latter simply being better Greek, in either case the point is that Jesus is the occasion and place where the Spirit is encountered.

In his résumé of the usual presentation of Christian baptism in the New Testament, G. B. Caird observes the close connection between baptism and the gift of the spirit of God: "The case of Cornelius, in which the Spirit came first and baptism followed (Acts 10:47-48), was an exception to the normal pattern (Acts 2:38) that the Spirit followed baptism."[18]

Those two cases, in Cornelius's house and in Jerusalem at Pentecost, embrace the overall model of baptism as presented within the Book of Acts, the principal source for the practice within the earliest church. The first instance Caird mentions, the baptisms authorized by Peter in the house of the Roman officer Cornelius (Acts 10) represents the principle of the Petrine extension of activity far outside Jerusalem.[19] The other reference is the famous scene of the mass baptisms (of some three thousand people, according to Acts 2:41) following the events at Pentecost.

But before the contrast between those two scenes can be assessed, the underlying unity of their account of what baptism into Jesus' name involves needs to be appreciated. In each case, the principal agent of baptism, and the person who provides the theology to account for the practice and the attendant experience, is Peter. And the theological account he provides is quite coherent as one moves in order from Acts 2 to Acts 10.

At Pentecost, the spirit is portrayed as descending on the twelve apostles (including the newly chosen Matthias), and they speak God's praises in the various languages of those assembled from the four points of the compass for that summer feast of harvest, both Jews and proselytes (Acts 2:1-12). The mention of proselytes (2:11) and the stress that those gathered came from "every nation under heaven" (2:5) clearly point ahead to the inclusion of non-Jews by means of baptism within Acts.[20] But even Peter's explanation of the descent of the spirit does that. He quotes from the prophet Joel (3:1–5 in the Septuagint),

"And it will be in the last days, says God, that I will pour out from my spirit upon all flesh."[21]

"All flesh," not only historic Israel, is to receive of God's spirit.

Pentecost is the most notable feast (in calendrical terms) of Peter and his circle. Seven weeks after the close of the entire festival of Passover and Unleavened Bread came the feast called Weeks or Pentecost (in Greek, referring to the period of fifty days that was involved; see Lev. 23:15-22; Deut. 16:9-12). The waving of the sheaf before the LORD at the close of Passover anticipated the greater harvest (especially of wheat; see Exod. 34:22) that was to follow in the summer, and that is just what Weeks celebrates (so Lev. 23:10-15). The timing of the coming of the Holy Spirit in the recollection of Peter's circle is unequivocal (Acts 2:1-4), and the theme of Moses dispensing of the spirit on his elders is reflected (see Num. 11:11-29). The association of Weeks with the covenant with Noah (see *Jubilees* 6:1, 10-11, 17-19) may help to explain why the coming of spirit then was to extend to humanity at large (see Acts 2:5-11). First fruits were celebrated at Weeks (see Num. 28:26) and they are used to express the gift of spirit and resurrection in Paul's theology (Rom. 8:23; 11:16; 1 Cor. 15:20, 23). We should expect such connections with the Pentecostal theology of Peter in one of Peter's students (see Gal. 1:18), as we should expect him to be especially concerned to keep the feast of Pentecost (see 1 Cor. 16:8; 20:16) despite what he said about calendrical observations in Galatians (see Gal. 4:9-10; cf. 2:14).

Now we are in a position to see why it was natural within the Petrine circle to speak of baptism "into the name of Jesus": the cultic language was inspired by the environment of Pentecost. Those who entered into a fresh relationship to God by means of the Holy Spirit were themselves a kind of "first fruits" and found their identity in relation to Christ or spirit as "first fruit" (so Rom. 8:23; 11:16; 16:5; 1

Cor. 15:20, 23; 16:15; James 1:18; Rev. 14:4). The wide range of that usage, which attests the influence of the Petrine theology, reflects the deeply Pentecostal character of primitive Christianity. Access to the covenant by means of the spirit meant that they entered sacrificially "into the name" (*eis to onoma*) of Jesus in baptism. Also within the Petrine circle, Eucharist was celebrated in covenantal terms when one broke bread and shared the cup "into the remembrance of" (*eis ten anamnesin*) Jesus, a phrase associated with covenantal sacrifice.[22] Both baptism and Eucharist are sacrificial in the Petrine understanding, and both intimately involve the spirit of God.

Hartman makes a similar point in regard to the continuing presence of spirit in his discussion of a famous passage for Paul (1 Cor. 12:12-13):

"For just as the body is one and has many members, but all the members of the body, being many, are one body, so is Christ. Because by one spirit we were all immersed into one body, whether Jews or Greeks, whether slaves or free, and we were all made to drink one spirit."

As Hartman observes:

> The last clause of the verse, "We were all made to drink of one Spirit," could as well be translated "We all had the one Spirit poured over us." The Spirit not only brought the baptised persons into the body of Christ, but also remains with them as a divine active presence.[23]

Spirit is understood to be the continuing medium of faithful existence in Christ, and for that reason it is as natural to associate it with Eucharist as with baptism. After all, Paul could also say that believers, like the Israelites, drank the same spiritual drink, which came from Christ (1 Cor. 10:4[24]), and that the Israelites went through their own immersion (1 Cor.10:2).

When Peter is speaking in the house of Cornelius in Acts 10, the spirit falls upon those who are listening, and those there with Peter who were circumcised were astounded "that the gift of the holy spirit has been poured even upon the nations" (10:44-45). The choice of the verb "to pour" is no coincidence: it is resonant with the quotation of Joel in Acts 2:17. Indeed, those in Cornelius's house praise God "in tongues" (10:46)[25] in a manner reminiscent of the apostles' prophecy at Pentecost, and Peter directs that they be baptized "in the name of Christ Jesus" (10:47-48). That is just the direction Peter gave earlier to his sympathetic hearers at Pentecost (2:37-38). Probably in the case of his speech at Pentecost, and more definitely in the case of his speech in the house of Cornelius, Peter's directions were in Greek, and we should understand that immersion or baptism is not in any general sense and that "Jesus" (*Iesous*) has entered the Greek language as a name for Yeshua. Christian baptism, immersion into the name of Jesus with reception of the Holy Spirit, was developed within the practice of the circle of Peter.

In aggregate, the two passages do not suggest any real dispute as to whether the gift of the spirit followed or preceded baptism into Jesus' name. The point is rather that belief in and baptism into him is connected directly to the outpouring of God's spirit. The apparent disruption of the usual model in Acts 10 is intended to call attention to the artificiality (from the point of view of the emergent Petrine theology) of attempting to withhold baptism from those who believe (as Peter actually says in 10:47).[26] Two questions immediately arise at this point. First, why would it have been so natural for Peter to have extended baptism to non-Jews on the basis of the outpouring of spirit, when he was still sensitive to the scruples of Judaism? (And that sensitivity is recorded by Paul, a contemporary witness, see Gal. 2:11-14.)[27] Second, where did Peter understand the new infusion of spirit to have derived from?

Those two questions have a single answer: the source of the spirit is Jesus as raised from the dead. In Peter's speech at Pentecost, Jesus, having been exalted to the right hand of God, receives the promise of the Holy Spirit from the father and pours it out on his followers (2:33). The spirit that is poured out, then, comes directly from the majesty of

God, from his rule over creation as a whole. This is the spirit as it hovered over the waters at the beginning of creation (Gen. 1:1), and not as limited to Israel. Because the spirit is of God, who creates people in the divine image, its presence marks God's own activity, in which all those who follow Jesus are to be included. Jesus' own program had involved proclaiming God's kingdom on the authority of his possession of God's spirit (Matt. 12:28; Luke 11:20). Now, as a consequence of the resurrection, Jesus had poured out that same spirit upon those who would follow him. Baptism in the spirit (see Acts 1:4-5) and baptism into the name of Jesus were one and the same thing for that reason. That was why, as Hartman suggests, believing that Jesus was God's Son and calling upon his name were the occasions on which the spirit was to be received.[28] In the new environment of God's spirit that the resurrection signaled, baptism was indeed, as Matthew 28:19 indicates, an activity and an experience that involved the Father (the source of one's identity), the Son (the agent of one's identity), and the Holy Spirit (the medium of one's identity).

Because the spirit in question is God and Jesus' at one and the same time, the range of its results is extremely broad. It is as manifest as God's own creativity and as personal as an individual believer's conviction. That was skillfully brought out by Charles Gore in a study that still merits careful consideration:

> It is true that St. Luke lays stress on the wonderful signs which marked the sudden arrival of the Spirit on, or just before, the day of Pentecost and on the similar signs which marked the first bestowal of the gift upon the Gentiles, Cornelius, and his companions and again on the twelve men who had been disciples of John the Baptist and were now led on into the faith of Christ.[29] And he delights to recount the miracles of healing wrought by the apostles. But also courage in speaking the word, and wisdom, and faith, and large-hearted goodness are associated with the Spirit's presence,[30] and He is recognized not only as the inspirer of the prophets of old, but also as the present and personal guide and helper

of individuals, and of the assemblies of the Church, in all their ways.[31]

Gore's observation is worth stressing, because there is a persistent tendency, even in otherwise well-informed circles, to limit unduly the place of spirit in earliest Christianity. One scholarly book refers to Acts 2 and then to Paul's well-known caution about spiritual gifts in 1 Corinthians 14 and goes on to state, "We hear nothing further concerning spirit possession in the early Church for another century."[32]

A commonly held view has that Christianity is not a religion emphasizing spirit, so when people claim God's spirit possesses them, that is an unusual occurrence. When a movement is styled "Pentecostalist" in the current religious scene, that designation is used to characterize the group concerned as outside of the mainstream of Christianity. But the scene of Pentecost and the scene in the house of Cornelius together demonstrate that possession by God's spirit was understood to be fundamental to faith in Jesus and was the principal element in the experience of baptism in the name of Jesus.

Gore also perceived that Paul was deeply influenced by this understanding of the spirit, an understanding (as we will see below) derived from the teaching of Peter regarding resurrection, baptism, and the spirit. The result is that, in Paul's letters "'in the Spirit' also means 'in Christ.'" Gore is rather tentative in regard to explaining the reason for this usage:

> We cannot speak with any confidence as to how precisely this conception was formed in St. Paul's mind. I suppose that the actual experience of the Church, before St. Paul came on the scene, had given the apostles and their companions an intense sense, as of the personal Christ now glorified in the heavens, so also of the personal Spirit, the Spirit of Jesus, guiding them from within. I suppose also that from the first they must have realized that the Holy Spirit was something more than the substitute for a now absent Christ.[33]

When we recall Paul's confident statement that baptism is when the spirit of God's own son cries "Abba! Father!" as in the case of Jesus (so Gal. 4:6), Gore's hesitation may seem difficult to understand. Evidently, he was influenced by the notion that the spirit was somehow an unusual conception within earliest Christianity.

In fact, however, the association of the Holy Spirit with baptism is well attested as a principal element of earliest Christian faith. Its roots are as deep as the teaching within the circle of Peter that, since Jesus has been exalted in his resurrection, he is in a position to pour out from the spirit that had been within him on those who believe in his name (see Acts 2:30-42). Owing to Peter's influence, that conviction was passed on to Paul, who was catechized by Peter around the year 35 C.E.[34]

But beyond Paul, we also see baptism in water and the spirit portrayed in terms of a new birth in the Gospel according to John (3:1-8). That shows the extent to which the basic understanding of baptism into Jesus' name as the occasion of receiving spirit was developed further in John on the basis of the kind of teaching we also encounter in the Synoptic Gospels (under the form of Jesus' own baptism). The first letter of Peter (related only derivatively to the teaching of Peter himself[35]) demonstrates a considerable development of the same theme. God is praised as "the God and father of our Lord, Christ Jesus" for "begetting us anew for a living hope through the resurrection of Christ Jesus from the dead" (1 Pet. 1:3). The theme of this letter, and of this passage in particular (1 Pet. 1:3-12), is that holding fast to the treasure of baptism will bring "the salvation of your souls" (1 Pet. 1:9), and that involves an awareness that what is announced to Christians was hidden even to prophets in times past (1 Pet. 1:10-11). Now, however, that is disclosed by "Holy Spirit sent from heaven" (1 Pet. 1:12), which is also "Christ's Spirit" (1 Pet. 1:11).

That close identification between Christ's spirit and the spirit of God, characteristic of Paul's letters as well as of First Peter, is also vividly portrayed in the Gospel according to John. There, it is precisely the risen Jesus who bestows the Holy Spirit on his disciples, when they

73

are gathered together in a closed room (20:19-22). The portrayal in this Gospel, produced at the turn of the first and second centuries, is profoundly theological in its reflection of the identification of Christ and spirit. The fact that Jesus comes after the doors have been closed "on account of fear of the Jews" (20:19) establishes that he comes only to the disciples and to no one else. Moreover, the substance of his body is quite obviously not ordinary human flesh; implicitly, John accepts the Pauline analysis that the body of the resurrected Jesus was spiritual, not carnal (see 1 Cor. 15:35-49[36]). Once in the room, limited to his own, Jesus breathes on them and says to them, "Receive the Holy Spirit" (20:22). That statement is so laconic that its profound significance might all too easily be overlooked: Jesus personally, from his own resurrected body, breathes Holy Spirit on his followers.

It has been frequently been remarked in the history of discussion that both the Holy Spirit and prophecy were widely understood to have ceased from Israel by the first century.[37] In that context, John 20:22 is startling for two reasons. First, the very presence of spirit, and indeed God's own spirit ("Holy Spirit"), marks the dawn of a new age. That is spelled out in Acts 2 by means of its reference to the Book of Joel and is conveyed by the drama of Jesus' personal action in John. Second, the identification between Jesus and the spirit, already accomplished in Acts 2, is deeply personalized in John 20. Here, the body of the risen Jesus conveys to the disciples the power of spirit, the power to forgive. For that reason, Jesus can here say, "Just as the father send me, so I send you" (20:21).

Paul had already been familiar with the idea that "by the name of our Lord Christ Jesus and by the spirit of our God" forgiveness had been granted in baptism (1 Cor. 6:11). But John takes a step beyond that common theology and finishes the scene in the closed room by having Jesus give his disciples the authority to forgive and to confirm sins (20:23). That is an emphatic statement in John, which contradicts the presentation in Matthew (composed around the year 80 C.E.), where Jesus—equally emphatically—delegates that authority during his ministry (to Peter in Matt. 16:19 and to his disciples in

18:18), not after his resurrection. The reason for this contradiction[38] is plainly provided in John: the spirit is only given after Jesus has been glorified (7:37-39):

"On the last, great day of the feast [of Sukkoth, or Tabernacles, see 7:2], Jesus stood and cried out, saying, 'If anyone thirst, let one come to be and drink. Who believes in me, just as Scripture says, fountains of living water will flow out of his belly.' But he said this about the spirit, which those who believed in him were going to receive; for there was no yet spirit, because Jesus had not been glorified."

In his study of the fourth Gospel, John Ashton has clearly shown that this final statement is a governing theme, tightly linked to the sending of the disciples in 20:21-22.[39] It is only the risen Jesus who can give the spirit which is intimately identified with his own person and teaching, because he can function in his divine status only as glorified.[40]

Acts may be said to be the story of the outward moving impact of the spirit from its center in Jerusalem. Once the inclusion of non-Jews is accepted, those who are associated with Paul and Barnabas in Antioch (named as Symeon called Niger, Lucius of Cyrene, and Manaen, an associate of Herod Antipas[41]), as well as those apostles themselves, are said to be directed by the spirit (Acts 13:1-4; 16:6-10; 20:28). Paul becomes the principal agent of baptism and the spirit, once the field of mission is far from Antioch, and it is from his perspective that the story of Apollos's ministry in Ephesus and Corinth is told (Acts 17:24–18:7). Apollos teaches only what is called the baptism of John, although Priscilla and Aquila correct him. But the definitive correction occurs when Paul comes to Ephesus, and those who had been baptized into John's baptism are now baptized into Jesus' name and receive the Holy Spirit when Paul lays his hands on them.[42]

Jerome Murphy-O'Connor has suggested that the reason for distinctive practices of baptism within primitive Christianity was that some followers of Jesus continued his practice while he was a disciple of John's, while most understood baptism as redefined by those who knew "the Risen Lord."[43] That distinction is crucial for an understanding of the literary program of Acts and of the practice of baptism after the resurrection of Jesus. The spirit, as released in baptism into the name of Jesus, is what distinguishes the practice of the church from the practice of Jesus, and what explains why the movement that had defined itself during Jesus' life by desisting from baptism now made baptism its emblem. The contrast the risen Jesus makes in Acts is instructive (Acts 1:5):

"John indeed baptized with water, while you will be baptized in Holy Spirit."

What is marked here is not only a periodization in time, of the resurrection as the caesura between immersing for purity and baptizing into Jesus' name; a change in the actual medium of baptism is also marked. The medium in John's immersion was water, because the issue was purification; the medium of baptism into the name of Jesus is spirit, because the issue is the empowerment that the spirit brings. As the risen Jesus goes on to say in Acts 1:8:

"But you will receive power when the Holy Spirit has come upon you, and you will become my witnesses both in Jerusalem and all Judaea and Samaria, even to the end of the earth."

That, of course, articulates a major theme within the Gospel according to Luke and within Acts. At the same time, it expresses the theology of God's spirit that explains the activity of Peter after the resurrection.

The conviction that God's spirit could bring about resurrection is already attested in the Book of Ezekiel, when, in a famous vision, the LORD states he will cause spirit to enter dry bones in order to make them live (Ezek. 37:5). That wording is recalled in the Eighteen Benedictions, an ancient prayer of the synagogue whose roots reach into the first century.[44] The association of spirit and being raised from the dead was, therefore, well attested by the time of Jesus' resurrection. Within the circle of Peter, as we have seen on the evidence of Acts, that association was the very foundation of the life of the church, and the Petrine experience and teaching concerning God's spirit and its availability by baptism into the name of Jesus became a fundamental characteristic of Christianity.

Indeed, even the link between resurrection and water in Peter's theology is easier to understand on the basis of early Judaic theology. The Eighteen Benedictions allude not only to Ezekiel but also to Isaiah. The reference in Isaiah 26:19 to God's "dew of light" was widely understood to signify how he would raise the dead. This is clearly brought out in the Aramaic Targum of Isaiah (26:19):

> *You are he who brings* alive the dead, *you raise the bones of their* bodies. *All who were thrown in the* dust *will live* and sing *before you!* For your dew is a dew of light *for those who perform your law,* and *the wicked to whom you have given might, and they transgressed against your Memra, you will hand over to Gehenna.* [45]

Just as the Eighteen Benedictions allude to both Ezekiel 37:5 and Isaiah 26:19, so here, in the Aramaic rendition of Isaiah 26:19, the "bones" of Ezekiel 37 make their appearance. Spirit, God's luminous "dew," and resurrection were already linked in the eschatology of early Judaism and formed a vital precedent of Peter's experience of the resurrection of Jesus.

Although Simon Peter is clearly portrayed as the principal witness of Jesus' resurrection within the New Testament (see Luke 24:34 and 1 Cor. 15:5), there is only one narrative in the canon that portrays his experience of the risen Jesus. John 21 is widely agreed to be an addendum to the fourth Gospel and only derivatively related to Peter,[46] and yet its utility for understanding the Petrine theology of resurrection may not be discounted. Here, Peter and six other disciples are fishing on the Sea of Galilee, and Jesus appears on the shore unrecognized, asking if they have anything to eat. They have not caught anything all night, but at Jesus' command they cast their net and catch more fish than they can pull up.[47] The disciple whom Jesus loves recognizes Jesus and informs Peter who the stranger is. Peter leaps into the water and swims to shore, followed by the others in the boat. Jesus, whose identity none dares to ask, directs the preparation of breakfast from the 153 large fish that were caught. Finally, Peter himself is commissioned to shepherd the flock of Jesus.

Although this third appearance of the risen Jesus in John is the only appearance that features Peter,[48] the allusions to baptism and the direction of the church make it clear that it is far from the sort of tradition that would have been formed in any immediate proximity to Peter's experience. Still, one feature stands out. As in the story of what happened near and at Emmaus (which holds the place of an appearance to Peter in Luke 24:13–35), Jesus is not immediately known; his identity is a matter of inference (see John 21:7, 12 and Luke 24:16, 31). This, of course, is just the direction all of the Gospels are *not headed* in by their structuring of traditions. They anticipate an instantly recognizable Jesus, fully continuous with the man who was buried: that is the point of the story of the empty tomb in all four Gospels. The earlier, Petrine understanding of resurrection allows for a discontinuity between the risen Jesus and Jesus prior to his death, just as it makes room for the influence of the Holy Spirit on those who experience Jesus as alive after his execution.

Just as Peter's leaping into the water in John 21 is redolent of baptism into the name of Jesus, so is this moment the completion of the baptismal imagery articulated early in the Gospel. In his nocturnal discussion with Rabbi Nicodemus, Jesus says, "Unless one is born from water and Spirit, one cannot enter into the kingdom of God" (John 3:5). By the Johannine definition, that obvious prophecy of baptism can not be realized during Jesus' life, but only after Jesus' glorification, when spirit becomes available (see John 7:37-39 and the discussion above). Now that Jesus has breathed the Spirit on his followers (so John 20:22), the Spirit has been released, and such a new birth is possible. John 21 attests the connection among Spirit, baptism, and resurrection within the circle of Peter, even as it completes the promise of Jesus in John 3:21.[49]

Fortunately, there is an additional confirmation of the Petrine theology of resurrection and Spirit. Paul, who had himself studied with

Peter (see Gal. 1:18), not only refers to Peter as the principal witness of the resurrection (1 Cor. 15:5) but also opens his letter to the Romans with what is widely agreed to be a primitive statement of Jesus' identity (Rom. 1:1-4):

"Paul, Jesus Christ's slave, called an apostle—separated for God's message, which he declared beforehand through his prophets in holy scriptures concerning his son, came from David's seed according to flesh, designated God's Son in power according to Spirit of sanctity, by resurrection of the dead, Christ Jesus our Lord."

Jesus' resurrection and Jesus' designation as God's Son together are attested and enabled by the spirit of God. That is a founding principle of Christianity.

Paul, for all the controversy he occasioned, is a representative teacher of the primitive church when it concerns the Spirit of God. He understands that the Spirit of sonship that raised Jesus from the dead is also available to Jesus' followers in baptism (Rom. 8:14-16):

"For as many as are led by God's Spirit, they are God's sons. Because you did not receive a spirit of slavery again, for fear, but you received a spirit of sonship, by which we cried out, Abba, Father! The spirit itself testified with our spirit that we are God's children."

For Paul, as for the earliest Christians of the Petrine tradition, creation itself longed for the fulfillment of God's spirit, because God was making the world anew with a new people (see Rom. 8:22-23), and it had begun with the resurrection of his own Son.

What had begun with the immersion of John and his disciple Jesus, practiced for the purpose of purification, had become something new and distinctive and—within the practice of Christian faith—absolutely fundamental. Baptism now was into Jesus' name for the reception of the Holy Spirit. God's presence was so intimate and commanding, what happened amounted to a "new creation" (so Paul in Gal. 6:15-16). Moreover, the principle of contagious, healing purity—which had emerged in Jesus practice—was consciously taken up in the life of the church after the resurrection.

However broad and generally available the Holy Spirit in apostolic baptism was understood to be, its miraculous power as coming from God is underscored in Acts. By laying on hands, Ananias heals Paul (Acts 9:17-18), Paul himself heals on the way to Rome (Acts 28:8), and Peter raises Tabitha (Acts 9:41) in a manner which recalls Jesus' raising of the young woman (*talitha*) who was Jairus's daughter (Mark 5:43), all because the creative power of God was at work. To be immersed into Jesus' name was also to be drenched with the outpouring of God's Spirit and the social and natural and supernatural changes in the understanding of purity that that involved.

Conclusion

God is understood to disclose himself as endemically human in the *logos*. That conception of Jesus was developed in Christianity by the deployment of language that was traditional in Judaism and transformed. The issue of Spirit is radically distinctive from the conception of Islam, but, of course, the same historical relationship in the use of language does not apply. Instead, the Qur'an purports to state "that which was revealed to Abraham, Ishmael, Isaac, Jacob, and the tribes" as well as to "Moses, Jesus, and the prophets" (Al 'Imran, 3:84).

Rhetorically, this assertion might be compared with the relationship between Moses and Christ developed in the Sermon on the Mount (in a section called the Antitheses, Matt. 5:21-48). The logic of the Qur'an, however, uses the rhetoric of fulfillment in order to convey its message as the culmination of all prophetic revelation.[50] In the case of Christianity, God's Spirit is portrayed as acting in believers in ways that might even exceed the capacity of Jesus (by way of summary of the pattern traced in Part II, see John 14:12).

William Graham's characterization of Islam's response to religious difference might be generalized to include other perspectives:

What is particularly important to remember is that so long as Muslims were dealing with other religious minorities, apart from overt polytheists, *within* their own Muslim-ruled states, legal toleration was the norm and communal strife remained minimal. This is especially true if one compares the situation of Jews and Christians in Muslim states with that of Jews and Muslims in Christian states in the same periods. Of course, border areas were a special case. In these, Muslim populations were typically threatened by non-Muslim states close by, and warfare with these non-Muslim states was frequent. As a result, toleration had a harder time flourishing in these contexts, as one would expect in any similar situation anywhere.[51]

These comments reflect circumstances that have, in recent years, pressed comparative theology to a new task. Tolerance and mutual respect among religions, particularly the Abrahamic religions, has emerged as an imperative for peace and form some communities as a necessity for survival. Perhaps theologians should embrace that social impetus and involve themselves constructively in the celebration of the same God as the inheritance of Abraham.

Daniel Boyarin has criticized just this suggestion in his historical assessment of Judaism and Christianity. He has shown that the two religions should not be understood as parting from one another at any finite moment. Indeed, he challenges the use of "religion" to characterize Rabbinic Judaism at all, arguing that Christian apologists developed this category in order to dispute allegedly restrictive Jewish views.[52] His argument extends an insight that he developed in a study of Paul:

Paul's genius was not as a philosopher, which he was not, but in his realization that the common dualist theology—ontology, anthropology, and hermeneutics—which together for him formed a Christology, provided the answer to the theological problem that troubled him the most: How do the rest of the people in God's world fit into the plan of salvation revealed to the Jews through their Torah?[53]

My understanding of Paul, directed by his own biography as well as with most exegetical opinion, makes his orientation more specifically Stoic than Boyarin suggests. I have also argued that Paul's background in Tarsus, and within a Hellenistic synagogue, helps account for his devotion to the international vocation of Israel, a vocation reinforced by apocalyptic influences that later shaped his thinking.[54] In other words, Paul's devotion to a unitary ideal in both theology and anthropology was consonant both with his Hellenistic and with his Judaic identity.

Although I disagree with Boyarin in the etiology of unitary perspectives, because I see them more as endemic within monotheisms (and philosophical henotheisms) than as specific to Christian thinkers, I agree with him that their inevitable tendency is apologetic. To declare that God is the "same" implicitly lays a claim to a superior definition of what makes for that sameness. (A comparable paradox has seen ecumenical progress thwarted by the formation of groups that claim to be more inclusive than any others, but then set up separate identities and so promote more faction.) As an analytic category in the comparative study of religion and theology, "sameness" does not appear productive.

But allowing Christianity, Islam, and Judaism their distinctive characters, without a program of discovering sameness, does not obviate confronting their competition with one another. Comparison makes that competition seem all the more acute. They compete not only over whose God was disclosed to Abraham, but over the *who* that God truly is, as revealed to whom, with the demands of what kind of justice, and by the sanction of what eternal rewards and punishments.

Systematic comparison sometimes points to moments when one of the Abrahamic religions appears at odds with the other two. Christianity's Incarnation, Islam's seal of prophecy, and Judaism's eternal Israel are as unacceptable to their partners as they are nonnegotiable to faith as articulated in canonical and classic literatures. Each partner can learn from the others, because they share categories of faith, even as they differ from one another in what is believed. But precisely because they all lay claim to the one God of Abraham, contradiction must attend their interactions. Each of the Abrahamic religions, while asserting that God is unique, also insists that its identification of God is uniquely true. That is why their God is one and not the same, and why believers need to acquire a taste for the fruits of difference.

The Ethiopian's Dilemma: Islam, Religious Boundaries, and the Identity of God

Vincent J. Cornell

The Ethiopian's Dilemma

The title of this essay refers to one of the most famous episodes in the early history of Islam. A few years after the Prophet Muhammad began preaching the message of Islam in Mecca, the oppression of the pagans against the Muslims became so severe that he was forced to send many of his followers, including his daughter Ruqayya and her husband the future Caliph 'Uthman, to Ethiopia as refugees. Upon their departure the Prophet told the refugees, "You should go to Abyssinia, for its king will not tolerate injustice, and it is a friendly country."[1] The Arabic term for the king of Abyssinia was *al-Najashi*, which comes from *nagasha*, a word that means "ruler" in the Tigrean language. In English this title is rendered as "Negus." Evidence from Islamic traditions and historical sources have allowed modern scholars to identify this king as Ellá Seham, who ruled as Negus of the Christian state of Aksum in the first decades of the seventh century.

The story goes on to relate that the pagan leaders of Mecca sent a delegation to Abyssinia to request the return of the Muslim refugees. Before making his decision, the Negus called both groups together in his council to inquire about the new religion that the Muslims were accused of having invented. Ja'far ibn Abu Talib (d. 629), the Prophet Muhammad's cousin and elder brother of the future Caliph 'Ali, was the leader of the refugees. He responded to the Meccans' accusations, detailing the beliefs of Islam and quoting from the recently revealed *Surat Maryam*, or Chapter of Mary in the Qur'an.[2] After hearing Ja'far's explanation of Islam, the Negus replied, "In truth, this and what Jesus brought have come from the same source."[3] Then he reaffirmed his protection of the Muslims. The next day the Meccans returned to the council and accused the Muslims of slandering Jesus by calling him a slave. When the Negus inquired about this, Ja'far replied, "We say about [Jesus] that which our prophet brought, saying, he is a slave of God (*'abd Allah*). [But he is also God's] Messenger, and His Spirit, and His Word, which he cast into Mary the Blessed Virgin." After hearing this the Negus held up a stick and exclaimed: "By God, Jesus the Son of Mary does not exceed what you have said by the length of this stick!"[4] In another version of the story, the Negus draws a line in the sand with the stick and says: "The difference between you and me is the width of this line." Years later, after the refugees had returned to Arabia and the Prophet Muhammad established the first Islamic state in Medina, word came that the Negus of Abyssinia had died. Upon hearing this news, the Prophet ordered a funeral prayer to be held for him *in absentia*, just as if he had been a Muslim.

Most Muslims believe that the Negus embraced Islam in secret. Muhammad ibn Ishaq (d. 773), the author of the earliest biography of the Prophet Muhammad, claimed that Ellá Seham's people accused him of heresy for supporting Islam and tried to revolt against him.[5] Today there is even a website in his memory (www.al-najashi.org) that is devoted to promoting better Muslim-Christian relations. However, Ethiopian sources do not state that the Negus was a crypto-Muslim or that he ever gave up his Christianity. If this had been the case, it would probably have been mentioned in historical sources or his name would have been erased from the lists of the kings of Ethiopia.

As a Muslim scholar of Islamic Studies, I have always felt that instead of claiming that the Negus was a Muslim, Muslims would benefit more from reflecting on the wisdom of the statements attributed to him. His statements, "This and what Jesus brought have come from the same source," and "Jesus the Son of Mary does not exceed what you have said by the length of this stick," are astute observations on the nature of the doctrinal differences between Islam and Christianity. Although the Negus draws attention to the fact that the two religions come from the same source and the overall extent of the differences between Islam and Christianity is small, he does not deny the existence of difference itself. In this sense his statements remind me of another famous saying by Gerald Burrill, who served as Episcopal Bishop of Chicago between 1954 and 1971: "The difference between a rut and a grave is the depth." When taken together, these three statements articulate a problem that I will call the Ethiopian's Dilemma in honor of the Negus. Despite the many similarities between Christianity and Islam, these similarities have not been sufficient to create a lasting sense of concord between the two religions. From a distance the differences between Christianity and Islam seem as small as the length of a stick or the width of a line in the sand. However, on closer observation these differences can become deal breakers.

The most important deal breakers between Christianity and Islam are the doctrines of the Trinity and Christology, the doctrine of the identity of Christ as embodied in the Incarnation of Jesus of Nazareth as the Son of God.[6] Belief in the Trinity and Christology constitute the theological essence of what it means to be a Christian. One cannot truly call oneself a Christian without believing in some form of these doctrines. Yet the Qur'an denies both of them. Likewise, acceptance of the Qur'an as the revealed Word of God constitutes the essence of what it means to be a Muslim. No person can truly call herself Muslim and reject the teachings of the Qur'an.

In Islam the doctrine of the Trinity is contradicted by the theology of *tawhid*, the doctrine of divine simplicity and the Oneness of God. The Qur'an states unambiguously: "Those who say, 'Verily God is a third of three,' have denied the truth (*laqad kafara*), for there is no God but One God" (Qur'an 5:73).[7] On Christology the Qur'an is equally unambiguous: "Those who say that God is the Messiah the Son of Mary deny the truth" (Qur'an 5:72). The Qur'an also states: "They (i.e., the Christians) say, 'God has begotten a son, glory be to Him!' Nay, to [God] belongs all that is in the heavens and the earth. Everything renders worship unto Him" (Qur'an 2:116). As for the person of Jesus of Nazareth, although he is highly revered in Islam as a prophet, he is still a mortal human being: "The Messiah Son of Mary is no more than a Messenger like the Messengers before him" (Qur'an 5:75). The contradiction between the Christian doctrines of the Trinity and Christology and the Islamic doctrine of *tawhid* is a classic illustration of the Ethiopian's Dilemma. Despite the many similarities that exist between Christianity and Islam, because of a few crucial theological differences Gerald Burrill's rut has most often been a grave and the length of the Negus's stick might as well be as long as a mile.

The Ethiopian's Dilemma is also a reminder of the danger of ignoring creedal boundaries between religions. The purpose of a religious creed is to draw a doctrinal line in the sand that believers are not supposed to cross. By policing the limits of doctrine, creeds determine the official or semiofficial boundaries of orthodoxy, heresy, and apostasy. However, despite their specificity, religious creeds still leave important theological questions unanswered. How is one supposed to measure such lines in the sand: by their length, their width, or their depth? And what are scholars of religion supposed to make of creedal boundaries today, if we hope to cross them for the sake of religious peace and mutual understanding? Does the recent reassertion of creedalism in the Abrahamic religions mean that the liberal ideal of religious pluralism is a zero-sum game between unbelief and faith? In other words, are religious progressives or liberal pluralists bad believers? Those of us who teach religions comparatively often face the charge that our interest in other religions means that something is wrong with our own faith. As the late Oxford scholar of religion R. C. Zaehner remarked about the academic field of religious studies, "The less we believe, the more we talk about what other people believe."[8]

Many Muslims would agree with Zaehner that it is not necessary for a believer to care about what nonbelievers believe. Partly for this reason, in the world of Islam the Ethiopian's Dilemma has never been resolved. Although Muslims, Christians, and Jews have crossed each other's creedal boundaries from time to time, it has usually been in limited ways and in localized contexts. The attempt by Muslims to make the Negus of Abyssinia one of themselves is a tacit admission of the failure of Muslim-Christian relations. The state of Muslim-Christian relations still suffers today from the troubled legacy of Jihad and Crusade at one end of the spectrum and bare tolerance or principled indifference at the other. When Congresswoman Michelle Bachman conjures up fears of a Muslim Fifth Column in the U.S. State Department or when Boko Haram burns down churches in Nigeria and threatens to kill Christians if they do not convert to Islam, their actions may seem foolish or extreme, but the passions that inflame them go back to the earliest confrontations between Islam and Christianity. In the history of Muslim-Christian conflict theological polemics have been used as weapons nearly as often as the spear and the sword. Saint John of Damascus (d. 749) wrote one of the first Christian polemics against Islam in his book *The Fount of Wisdom*. Today the chapter of this book on the "Heresy of the Ishmaelites" (i.e., the Muslims) can be found on a Christian website, e-sword-users.org.

Although theological differences are not as significant between Islam and Judaism as they are between Islam and Christianity, the Ethiopian's Dilemma is also relevant to Muslim-Jewish relations. Ironically, the theological similarity between Judaism and Islam is part of the problem here. If Jews believe in God more or less the same way as Muslims do, then what is wrong with them? The most common answer to this question in Islam has revolved around the alleged behavior of the Jews as a community. The persistence of Judaism as an ethno-religious community poses a challenge to Islam's ideological and creedal notion of community, which is expressed in the concept of the *umma muslima*: the "mother" or paradigmatic community of believers in submission to God (Qur'an 2:143).[9] The Qur'an most often refers to the Jews as *Banu Isra'il*, "The Sons (or Children) of Israel."[10] This is essentially a tribal appellation. Bedouin Arab tribes also used the *Banu* or "Sons of" designation, as in the names of the tribes Banu Hilal or Banu Hanifa. Anthropologically, Middle Eastern tribes are extended families that trace their descent from a common ancestor. Likewise the Banu Isra'il are depicted as an extended family whose ethnic solidarity and dysfunctional behavior cause them to forget their responsibility to God. In *Surat al-Baqara* (The Discourse of the Cow, Qur'an 2), the Qur'an opens a long discourse on the Jews with a reminder to the Sons of Israel to fulfill the Covenant: "Oh Banu Isra'il! Remember the special favor that I (i.e., Allah) bestowed on you. So fulfill your Covenant with Me, that you may fulfill your covenant with yourselves" (Qur'an 2:40). The narrative goes on to recount the special favors that God bestowed on Israel, giving particular attention to the story of Moses and the resistance of his people to his leadership. Time and again they argue and bicker and demand more concessions from God through their prophet. Every time that God forgives them they break the Covenant again. *Surat al-Baqara* is named after the red heifer of Numbers 19:1–10 in the Pentateuch, which Moses and Aaron asked the Sons of Israel (this is also a biblical term) to sacrifice on God's behalf as expiation for their sins.[11] In the Qur'anic version of the story the people laugh at Moses and prevaricate by demanding additional stipulations before giving in to God's command (Qur'an 2:67-71).

Although in Islamic terms it is probably better to be criticized for bad behavior than for bad theology, the danger of treating a religious community as a tribe is that it can lead to the notion of collective guilt. This prejudice combined with the notion of a tribe as an extended family can also lead to racism, which in the case of the Jews is expressed as anti-Semitism. Taking Qur'anic critiques of the behavior of the Banu Isra'il as their cue, medieval Muslim polemicists tended to dismiss the

Jews as untrustworthy. Although they used to be God's chosen people, because of alleged defects in their character (variously described as learned or innate) they could not be expected to keep their word. In general, the line in the sand between Islam and Judaism was personal and associational rather than theological. For medieval Muslim polemicists, getting too close to the Jews meant that their bad traits might rub off on the Muslims. This notion of moral contagion can even be observed in the historical record. For example, in the fifteenth century the Moroccan Sufi and religious reformer Ahmad Zarruq (d. 1493) was cursed by his teacher to be mistaken for a Jew simply because he tried to defend the Jews during an uprising in the city of Fes.[12]

Certain Muslim regimes such as the Ismaili Shiite Fatimids of Egypt (tenth to twelfth century C.E.) and the Sunni Umayyads of Spain (eighth to eleventh century C.E.) were more tolerant of the Jews and even appointed Jews to high governmental positions. However, a grudging form of toleration punctuated by occasional periods of persecution was more commonly the rule. Also, because Jews were more common than Christians in most parts of the Muslim world, it was easier to turn them into scapegoats. In the ninth century the Muslim theologian and essayist Abu 'Uthman al-Jahiz of Baghdad (d. 869) remarked about Muslim-Jewish relations: "Man hates the one he knows, turns against the one he sees, opposes the one he resembles, and becomes observant of the faults of those with whom he mingles; the greater the love and intimacy, the greater the hatred and estrangement."[13]

Even the tolerant Fatimids, whose Muslim subjects lived among Jews in Cairo and formed business partnerships with them, used the theological doctrine of fulfillment to make Judaism appear the most primitive and backward of the Abrahamic religions. According to the doctrine of fulfillment each later revelation fulfills and replaces the revelation that came before it. An early Ismaili missionary text, *The Master and the Disciple* (*al-'Alim wa al-Muta'alim*), seems to suggest that for Jews the path to Islam should first go through Christianity. According to this work, since Christianity is the fulfillment of Judaism and since Islam is the fulfillment of Christianity, it is only logical that the Jews should come to Islam by way of Christianity.[14] The author of this text forgot, as most Muslims also forget today, that the Jews were the recipients of the only scripture other than the Qur'an to be referred to by the Qur'an itself as *al-Furqan*: the Law or Criterion of truth versus falsehood and unbelief: "We gave Moses and Aaron the Criterion (*al-Furqan*) and an inspiration and revelation for the God-fearing" (Qur'an 21:48). Rather than say that the Jews must pass through Christianity before coming to Islam, it is actually more Qur'anic to argue the opposite: Christians would come closer to Islam if they adhered to the Law that was revealed to Moses and Aaron.

Reform Theology: Supersession or Shared Spirituality?

The message of Islam as embodied in the Qur'an expresses a theology of reform. In the logic of reform theology there are three possible ways to frame the message of change. These possibilities are not mutually exclusive and the theology of a particular religion may include more than one of them. One possibility is to use the *logic of supersession*: the new religious teachings that come from the reform revelation are so different from previous doctrines or practices that they replace the old religion. This is the case of Christianity with respect to Judaism.[15] The doctrine of fulfillment referred to above is also part of the logic of supersession.

Another possibility is to base reform theology on the *logic of location*: the new religious teachings of the reform revelation are bestowed on a new people or on people who live in a different location from the recipients of the previous revelation. The most prominent example of the logic of location in contemporary Christianity is the case of Mormonism with respect to Catholicism and Protestantism. The revelation of *The Book of Mormon* to the prophet Joseph Smith is partly a reform of Christianity, but it is also a revelation given specifically to the people of America. This is a major reason why The Church of Jesus Christ of Latter-Day Saints includes a mission to the Native Americans.

The third possibility is to base reform theology on the *logic of restoration*: the religious teachings of the reform revelation are intended to restore the original but now corrupted teachings of the previous revelation. In Christianity, the mission of Jesus of Nazareth began as an attempt to restore the original spirit of Judaism. The teachings of Siddhartha or Gautama Buddha were meant in part to restore a corrupted Hinduism. The Mormon Church depicts itself as a restoration of the original Christian Church. The logic of restoration also applies to the Prophets of Israel, who came in different periods of history to lead their people back to God.

The logic of restoration is also central to the reform revelation of Islam, which seeks to restore the original monotheistic religion of Abraham and correct unwarranted doctrinal changes in the scriptures of the Pentateuch (Ar. *al-Tawrat*, the Torah) and the New Testament (Ar. *al-Injil*, "The Evangel"). In fact, all three approaches to reform theology can be found in Islam. The logic of location is used when the Qur'an depicts itself as God's revelation to the Arabs. The Qur'an often refers to itself as a revelation in Arabic. This can be observed in the following verse, which expresses both the logic of location and the logic of restoration: "And previously the Book of Moses (i.e., the Torah) was a guide and a mercy; this [Qur'an] is a book confirming [the Torah] in Arabic, so that it may warn those who are unjust and give good tidings to the righteous" (Qur'an 46:12). The logic of supersession is also used in Islam because truly submitting to God (the creedal meaning of the Arabic word *Islam*) means following the Qur'an and the Prophet Muhammad to the exclusion of all previous revelations and prophets. Verse 24:51 of the Qur'an states: "The answer of the believers when they are summoned to God and His Messenger so that he may judge between them is to say, 'We hear and obey.' It is these who will attain felicity." In Islamic jurisprudence (*fiqh*) this verse was understood to mean that the Law of Islam (*al-Shari'a*) superseded the laws (*shara'i*) of all previous religions, including Judaism and Christianity.

Among Muslims, there has long been a debate over which logic of reform theology should predominate. Proponents of political Islam have tended to favor the logic of supersession. Because they see the establishment of Islam as dependent on the establishment of an Islamic state, they view Islam as a system of laws and use the Qur'an to argue that since the Islamic way of life is embodied in the Shari'a, and since the Shari'a supersedes all previous legal systems, the logic of supersession should take precedence over other approaches to reform theology. When combined with the logic of restoration, which views the scriptures of Judaism and Christianity as corrupted texts (a doctrine known in Arabic as *tahrif*), this logic tends to rule out any meaningful sense of shared spirituality between Muslims, Christians, and Jews. Historically, this has led to the practice of toleration as principled indifference. This is justified in the following way: Since the scriptures of Judaism and Christianity are corrupted, Jews and Christians cannot know the true nature of God. Thus, what they believe is not only wrong but it is also potentially harmful to the faith of Muslims. Therefore, there is no benefit in knowing about the beliefs of Christians or Jews in detail. What the Qur'an, the Prophet Muhammad, and his Companions have stated about Judaism and Christianity is sufficient for Muslims to know about the real teachings of Jesus, Moses, Abraham, and the other prophets of the Judeo-Christian tradition.

The resort to principled indifference is linked to both politics and power. It was predominant in much of the Muslim world during the time of Islam's hegemony and it also characterizes much of the West's attitude toward Islam today. For example, after more than forty years of interaction between Islamic Studies scholars and educational and news organizations in the United States, most news reporters and the public are nearly as ignorant of Islam today as they were in the 1970s. This persistence of institutional ignorance cannot be accidental. A similarly dismissive attitude about Judaism and Christianity prevailed among Muslim jurists in the medieval period and can still be found among many so-called Muslim fundamentalists. A number of polemical "dialogues" between Muslims, Christians, and Jews can be found in manuscript collections in Europe, North Africa, and the Middle East. What is striking about these dialogues is how little desire there is to learn from or even listen to the other. They are most often dialogues of the deaf in which each party talks past each other. In encounters such as these, the logic of supersession clearly took precedence over the other approaches to reform theology.

In the El Escorial Library of Spain is an Arabic manuscript that reproduces such a "dialogue" between a Muslim jurisconsult (*mufti*) named Abu Sa'id ibn Lubb (d. 1381) and a Jew of Granada. In this encounter the Jew asks the jurist to resolve the following moral and theological dilemma: If a Jew is destined by God not to believe in Islam, how can God justify punishing him if his unbelief conforms to God's will? Neither party is really interested in what the other has to say. The Jew poses a rhetorical question based on a stereotypical view of Islamic fatalism and the Muslim responds by treating the Jew as insincere and hypocritical. In accordance with the Qur'anic image of the Jews described above, his response to the Jew is more ethical than theological. For Ibn Lubb, the Jew is a congenital disbeliever, who is destined for divine punishment because of his hypocrisy and intransigence. At the end of his response he likens the Jew to Abu Lahab, the pagan uncle of the Prophet Muhammad who was one of the most stubborn opponents of Islam (Qur'an, Sura 111).[16]

However, in other periods of Islamic history the logic of restoration took precedence over the logic of supersession and a greater sense of shared spirituality prevailed. Historians have begun to realize that one of the better periods for interreligious dialogue was the time of the Umayyad Caliphate, which ruled over the Middle East from Damascus between 661 and 750. During this early period of Islamic history Muslims sought the advice of Jews and Christians because they were a ruling minority but also because the Qur'anic message of continuity with the Torah and the New Testament still resonated with them. An example of shared spirituality in this period can be found in the remains of a church near Jerusalem called the Kathisma of the Virgin. This eight-sided church was a *martyrium* (Gr. "place of witnessing"), a monument that commemorated a holy person or event. The church was built around a stone (the Greek word *kathisma* means "seat") where the Virgin Mary was supposed to have rested on her way from Jerusalem to Bethlehem before giving birth to Jesus. The design of the church was similar to the Dome of the Rock, a much larger building that was built as an Islamic *martyrium* (Ar. *mashhad*) to commemorate the spot where the Prophet Muhammad ascended to heaven during his Night Journey.

In the Umayyad period a *mihrab* was added on the south side of the Kathisma Church to indicate the direction of Mecca. Next to the *mihrab* was a mosaic of palm trees. This mosaic commemorated the Qur'anic story of the Virgin Mary, who sought refuge during her pregnancy beneath a palm tree (Qur'an 19:23-26). We can be certain that the Umayyads did not intend to turn this church into a mosque because the space between the *mihrab* and the wall surrounding the stone where Mary rested was too small to hold the minimum number of forty people required for congregational prayers.[17] Instead, the *mihrab* was most likely added so that Muslim visitors to the site could perform their individual prayers. In other words, the Kathisma Church seems to have functioned as a dual-purpose *martyrium*. Muslims apparently thought that it was the place where the Virgin Mary sought refuge during her pregnancy, while Christians saw it as the place where Mary rested on her way to Bethlehem. The dual use of this church provided an important example of a local solution to the Ethiopian's Dilemma. Because the logic of restoration took precedence over the logic of supersession, Muslims could compromise with Christians and create a space of shared spirituality, despite the theology that divided them. The Kathisma Church was thus a place where the width of the line between Islam and Christianity was narrow enough to cross, at least temporarily.

A compromise between Muslims and Jews at the Temple Mount in Jerusalem provides another example of a solution to the Ethiopian's Dilemma in the Umayyad period. After the destruction of the Second Temple by the Romans in 70 C.E. and the suppression of the Bar Kokhba revolt in 136 C.E., Jews were forbidden from entering Jerusalem on pain of death. Byzantine Christian rulers only allowed the Jews to visit

Jerusalem once a year on the Ninth of Av, the Day of Lamentation. The Muslims reopened Jerusalem to Jewish settlement after they conquered the city in 637. At the beginning of the Prophet Muhammad's mission, Muslims prayed toward Jerusalem. Even after they turned their prayers toward Mecca, they continued to venerate Jerusalem as a sacred city and regarded the site of the Temple as a holy place. After the conquest of Jerusalem the Caliph 'Umar (r. 634–640) ordered the Al Aqsa Mosque to be constructed to commemorate the site of the Temple.[18] A Muslim history of Jerusalem written during the Fatimid period reports that for eighty years, from the time of 'Umar until well into the Umayyad period, the privilege of tending the lamps of the Al Aqsa Mosque was reserved for Jews.[19] This text also indicates that rituals possibly modeled on Jewish rites were performed at the Dome of the Rock on Mondays and Thursdays.[20] These rites involved anointing the rock with special oils and purifying the sacred site with incense. Once again, because the logic of restoration fostered a sense of shared spirituality between Muslims and Jews, the Ethiopian's Dilemma could be resolved on the Temple Mount by decreasing both the width and the depth of the line between Judaism and Islam. For a while at least, some Jews could cross over the line to share a sacred space that was controlled by Muslims but consecrated in memory of a history that they both shared.

The Ethiopian's Dilemma and the Concept of God

Although the logic of restoration helped provide a solution to the Ethiopian's Dilemma in Umayyad Jerusalem by creating spaces for shared spirituality between Muslims and Christians and Jews, it only solved part of the problem. The compromise at the Kathisma Church may have crossed the dividing lines of sacred history, but it could not cross the lines of theology. Although Christian and Muslim devotees visited this site for different reasons, both of their religions recognized the Virgin Mary and it made little difference to the creed of Islam whether or not Mary married Joseph or whether they stopped and rested on a rock near Jerusalem on their way to Bethlehem. However, the reason why early Christians built this church in the first place made a great deal of creedal difference. For Christians, the stone at the center of the Kathisma of the Virgin was holy not just because Mary sat on it, but because the "Mother of God" sat on it. The Kathisma stone was a *hierophany*, a place where the sacred became manifest through indirect contact with the divine fetus in Mary's womb. As a place of pious visitation, the Kathisma Church was similar to the Christian Church of the Holy Sepulcher and the Islamic Dome of the Rock in Jerusalem. The Kathisma stone, the rock of Golgotha in the Church of the Holy Sepulcher, and the stone at the center of the Dome of the Rock were all points of contact with the sacred. The Dome of the Rock was a hierophany because it provided the starting point for the Prophet Muhammad's ascent to heaven (*al-Mi'raj*) on the Night Journey and his encounter with God. In fact, the entire Temple Mount, including the Al Aqsa Mosque is a hierophany for Muslims. As the site of Solomon's Temple, God's presence is manifest over its entire surface.

At the Kathisma Church, Muslims and Christians shared a sacred space and partly shared a narrative that explained it, but they could not share the theological meaning that they gave to the narrative. The wall that separated the Islamic *mihrab* from the stone where Mary sat symbolized the theological boundary that separated the Islamic and Christian versions of her story. Although Muslims may have honored the stone as the place where Mary took refuge under the palm tree, they did not believe in Mary as Mother of God. Similarly, Christians would not have stopped at the Islamic *mihrab* because the Qur'anic story of Mary's refuge under the palm tree (the original meaning of *mihrab* is "place of refuge") is not part of the Christian tradition. Every act of interreligious accommodation brings up the question of boundaries. Although the Kathisma of the Virgin was a religious site, the compromise that allowed Muslims and Christians to share it was secular. At this site tolerance could exist only by keeping theology out of the discussion.

However, when it comes to the most important differences between Christianity and Islam, theology is the crux of the problem. To return to the Ethiopian's Dilemma: if the length of the Negus's stick symbolizes the historical distance between Islamic and Christian narratives of Jesus, Bishop Burrill's difference between a rut and a grave stands for the theological distance between the Islamic Son of Mary and the Christian Son of God. Is it even realistic to hope that the Ethiopian's Dilemma can be resolved in light of such major theological differences? The answer to this question may be yes, but not without serious implications. To answer this question in the affirmative would mean in effect that the concept of God in Islam, Christianity, and Judaism is more similar than different across all three religions.

The question of theological similarity also begs the question of verisimilitude raised by Jacob Neusner in his contribution to this volume. Is God in Islam, Christianity, and Judaism theologically the same across all three religions, or does God just seem the same? Can we assume, as Neusner does, that monotheism creates its own logic that forces us to acknowledge our worship of the same God despite our theological differences? I am not convinced that we can go this far and still remain true to our traditional creeds. To say that God in Judaism, Christianity, and Islam is essentially the same would be to say that the notion of divinity in the Abrahamic religions could be reduced theologically to a least common denominator. In effect, this amounts to an argument for the transcendent unity of Abrahamic religions. This is similar to the argument for the transcendent unity of religions that advocates of Perennial Philosophy make. Perennialists try to resolve the theological differences between religions by appealing to a higher metaphysics that transforms theological differences into questions of perspective, proportion, or context. The problem with this approach is that by viewing religious differences at too great a remove we run the risk of creating what Steven Wasserstrom has called "Religion after Religion."[21] In other words, we risk replacing our traditional creeds with a construct that bears little actual resemblance to what we find in our scriptures.

However, we must also be careful not to overdetermine the notion of difference by magnifying second-order differences in a fundamentalist way. Although the creedal boundaries between Judaism, Christianity, and Islam are important, there are compelling historical and theological reasons why the Abrahamic religions are distinct from other religions. The problem of determining which boundaries are necessary and which are supererogatory is one of the most important problems to be faced in solving the Ethiopian's Dilemma. Although the historical practice of theology has often been an apologetic or polemical enterprise, this does not have to be the case. I believe that in a postcolonial and globalized world the only adequate way to practice theology is to make it comparative, critical, and constructive. As Bruce Chilton points out in his essay for this volume, an uncritical theology of comparison can be hegemonic by claiming a superior definition of sameness. However, a constructive theology of Islam that is both comparative and (self)-critical could teach Muslims to view our faith in light of its rivals and help us gain a deeper and more nuanced understanding of God. This does not necessarily mean that we would have to abandon our traditional creeds completely but it does mean that we might have to revise them in certain places. The value of creeds is that they simplify and schematize the findings of theologians and turn them into rules and principles that believers can refer to in their spiritual lives. However, we must also be mindful that our existing creeds are the result of political considerations as much as of theological arguments.

From a logical point of view it would seem relatively easy for Muslims to say that Jews, Christians, and Muslims worship the same God. Muslims can afford to be theologically open-minded because Islam is the latest of the three Abrahamic religions historically and recognizes Christianity and Judaism as its predecessors. The Qur'an tells the Prophet Muhammad: "Say: 'We believe in Allah and what was revealed to us. [We also believe in] what was revealed to Abraham, Isaac, Jacob, and the Tribes, and that which was given to Moses and Jesus and all of the Prophets from their Lord. We make no distinctions between any of them; rather, we belong to [the Lord] in our submission'" (Qur'an 2:136). Even more significantly, the Qur'an instructs the Prophet to say to the People of the Book: "We believe in what was revealed to us and what was revealed to you. Our God and your God is one and we are all in submission to Him" (Qur'an 29:46). Although this verse might be construed as theologically hegemonic because the Qur'an sets its own rules of comparison when it comes to the definition of God, its logic is unassailable. Because Islam is a reform religion, the God of Islam must be the same in His original essence as the God of the other Abrahamic religions. If the God of Abraham is the God of Islam, and if the God of Abraham is the God of Judaism and Christianity, then all three religions share the same God of Abraham. Most Muslims see this as the meaning of the classic statement on Abraham in the Qur'an: "Abraham was neither a Jew nor a Christian but a primordial monotheist who submitted to God (*kana hanifan musliman*); and he was not one of the polytheists (*wa ma kana min al-mushrikin*)" (Qur'an 3:67).

Unfortunately many Muslims who consider Allah to be the God of Abraham do not believe that contemporary Jews and Christians worship Allah because the Qur'an says that Abraham was neither a Jew nor a Christian. Although I disagree with this opinion, it is not illogical. The key question in this case is what the Qur'an means by calling Abraham a "Muslim Hanif." The Qur'an itself does not define this term clearly and the historical record is also murky. The best that historians can come up with is that at the time of the Prophet Muhammad the term *hanif* referred to something like a free-range monotheist. The *hunafa'* (the Arabic plural of *hanif*) were ascetics in the Arabian Peninsula who worshiped the God of Abraham but refused to call themselves Jews or Christians.[22]

Two verses of the Qur'an state that the monotheism of the *hunafa'* is the natural religious disposition (*fitra*) for which God predisposed humankind (Qur'an 2:129-35 and 3:60-67). In virtually every instance in which the Qur'an uses the term *hanif*, it is strongly contrasted with the term *mushrik*, "one who associates with something or takes a partner." In Qur'an 3:67 above, the term for polytheists is *mushrikin*, the genitive plural of *mushrik*. Terminological contrasts such as these suggest that the *hunafa'* of Arabia were opponents of polytheism. However, the Qur'an also makes a point of distinguishing between the *hunafa'* and Jews and Christians, who were also opponents of polytheism. According to the

Qur'an, unlike the *hunafā'*, Jews and Christians abandoned the essential teachings of Abraham's religion and followed the errors of nations that went astray before them (Qur'an 5:77). Once again, however, the Qur'an is unclear about exactly what this means. Sometimes the errors of the Christians and Jews are portrayed as theological (Qur'an 5:78) but at other times they are portrayed as moral (Qur'an 5:79). The relationship between theological and moral errors remains an open question.

However, the Qur'an clearly states that God forgives all sins except *shirk*, associating partners with God (Qur'an 4:48). No one doubts that this ruling applies to the polytheists, but what about Christians? Are Christians polytheists too? Certain verses of the Qur'an seem to suggest that they are (cf. Qur'an 5:17). However, the Qur'an also says that Christians are the closest in sympathy to the Muslims and singles out Christian monks (Ar. *ruhban*) for special praise (Qur'an 5:82). In principle, the Qur'an supports the concept of religious freedom: "There is no compulsion in religion; true guidance is distinct from error" (Qur'an 2:256). It is impossible to overstate the importance of this verse to the Muslim practice of religious tolerance, despite the fact that tolerance in practice often fell short of modern liberal ideals. Other Qur'anic verses go even further and hold out the promise of salvation to Christians and Jews: "Verily those who believe [in Islam], and those who are Jews, Sabians, and Christians—any who believe in Allah and the Last Day and work righteousness—no fear shall be upon them, nor shall they grieve" (Qur'an 5:69). Islam is unique among the Abrahamic religions in opening the door of salvation to its monotheistic rivals. These verses alone are sufficient to condemn intolerant groups such as Boko Haram and Al Qaeda as extremists. Theologically these verses, along with other verses in the Qur'an that call on Jews and Christians to hold fast to the teachings of the Torah and the Gospel (Qur'an 5:68), suggest that a common conception of God does in fact exist within the Abrahamic religions and point toward a possible solution to the Ethiopian's Dilemma.

However, every time a solution to this dilemma seems to appear, a new problem takes its place. For example, the theological simplicity of the monotheistic concept of God may itself give rise to some of the issues that complicate the search for a solution to the Ethiopian's Dilemma. The problem with a theology of divine simplicity is that people often want to fill in the details. They forget that the very ambiguity of a theology of divine simplicity is a mercy from God. It is easier to conceive of a brotherhood of monotheistic religions when secondary theological questions are removed from the debate. However, the natural desire to say more about less creates new theological problems to be solved. This paradox is expressed in a poem by 'Abdallah al-Ghazwani (d. 1529), an important Sufi from Morocco. Although the poem is ostensibly about the theological problem of pantheism, it is also relevant to the Ethiopian's Dilemma because the resolution of religious differences involves a similar problem of discerning a common notion of God behind a multiplicity of theological formulations:

> Oh One of everything! Oh He for whom everything is One!
> The person behind the veil enumerates You, Oh One.
>
> You appeared in everything so that the One would not be hidden,
> But then you disappeared in everything such that the One could not
> appear![23]

We who are behind the veil of human experience cannot fully comprehend the God of All. However, because of questions that have been raised in churches, mosques, and synagogues, and because of provocative statements made by certain politicians and religious leaders, we are called upon to answer in a thin volume of essays a theological question that has perplexed scholars for centuries. Because of the limited state of our knowledge the very question of whether Jews, Christians, and Muslims worship the same God is (theo)-logically inappropriate. This question does not ask whether the theologies of Islam, Christianity, and Judaism are compatible with each other but rather whether the God of each religion is the *same God* as the God of the other.

For Jacob Neusner, the logic of monotheism compels us to answer this question in the affirmative. I would respond that when we personalize God and make God our possession, the concept of the monotheistic oneness of faith inevitably goes out the door and a plurality of fideistic notions arrives in its place. Fideists are not likely to consider the Ethiopian's dilemma as a problem worth solving. For Ghazwani, the problem of comprehending God theologically is that He makes Himself present everywhere so that He can be known, but at the same time the variety of the modes in which He reveals Himself conceals Him such that we cannot discern His Sameness. As in the old saying, we cannot see the forest for the trees. Thus, like a person with obsessive-compulsive disorder, we try to "enumerate" God in various ways: we assign Him names, attributes, persons, hypostases and other characteristics in order to convince ourselves that we can truly understand a Being that is beyond our comprehension.

However, while recognizing our intellectual limits as well as the need for greater openness toward other theological perspectives, we still have to draw boundaries around our beliefs because otherwise institutional religion would have no meaning. As R.C. Zaehner never hesitated to point out, a religion of all faiths is a religion of no faith at all. We have no choice but to draw lines in the sand and enumerate the attributes of God as we conceive Him by making theological formulations and creeds. We cannot help but conceptualize our beliefs in words. Thus, it is fitting that in Islam the term for theology is *'ilm al-kalam*: the "science of words." Another Sufi thinker who recognized the codependent relationship between human nature and words was Farid al-Din al-'Attar (d. 1221) of Nishapur in eastern Iran. In the introduction to the *Ilahi-Nama*, a book that discusses theology by means of stories and poems, he advises the reader:

> Do not look with the eye of contempt upon words, for both [this world and the hereafter] are filled with the single word, "Be!" The foundation of both worlds is nothing but words, for they were created with the word, "Be!" and can be destroyed with the words, "Be not!"[24]

For 'Attar our attempt to understand God through words is inevitable because all of existence, including the existence of ideas, is merely hypothetical until it is put into words. Just as the words of the Qur'an reflect the Divine Word in creation, so the creativity of human words is a reflection of the creative Word of God. In the final analysis, human beings cannot live without words. "Since words are the basis of everything," says 'Attar, "Do everything with words: beg with them, ask with them, and seek with them."[25]

In the remainder of this essay I will follow 'Attar's advice and see if a solution to the Ethiopian's Dilemma can be found within the "words" of Islamic theology. I will assume that in asking whether Muslims, Christians, and Jews worship the same God we are really asking, "Are Islam, Christianity, and Judaism compatible theologically?" As noted above, the answer that we give to this question has creedal implications. It also has social and moral implications. In effect we are asking: Is there room for the Abrahamic other within the theology of my religion? This is likely the same question that the Negus of Abyssinia asked himself when he judged the Muslim refugees: How far do I have to stretch the boundaries of my traditional beliefs to extend hospitality to the followers of this new religion? In attempting to answer this question I will rely primarily on the text of the Qur'an with the help of a few respected works of Jewish and Christian theology. In the first section that follows I will explore the theological compatibility between Islam and Judaism. In the next section I will explore the more problematical issue of theological compatibility between Islam and Christianity. Finally, I will conclude this essay with some personal observations on comparison and whether the Ethiopian's Dilemma can or cannot be resolved theologically.

Do Muslims and Jews Worship the Same God?

Theologically, any investigation of the Islamic side of the question of whether Jews, Christians, and Muslims worship the same God must begin with *Surat al-Kafirun* (Qur'an 109). This short Sura constitutes the Qur'an's line in the sand with respect to the ultimate object of religious worship. Although the Sura does not define the concept of unbelief per se, it makes it clear that there is a limit to theological compromise. Muslims have traditionally conceived of this limit according to the Islamic doctrine of *tawhid* or simple monotheism.

> Say: "Oh *kafirun*:
> I do not worship what you worship.
> Nor do you worship what I worship.
> Nor do I currently worship that which you used to worship.
> Nor do you currently worship what I worship.
> To you your religion and to me mine." (Qur'an 109)

The term *kafirun* in this Sura comes from the Arabic verb *kafara*, which means, "to deny," "to conceal," "to cover up." *Kafir* is the active participle of this verb and it is the most commonly used term for both "polytheist" and "unbeliever" in Islam. *Kafir* can also mean "denier" in a more general, nontheological sense. *Kafirun* is the plural of *kafir*. Significantly, out of the many instances in which some form of the verb *kafara* appears in the Qur'an, it is only rarely applied to Jews. In the few cases where this does occur, the verb describes how the Banu Isra'il or the "People of the Book" (*ahl al-kitab*) denied the Prophets and Messengers that were sent to reform them. This is an example of the nontheological use of the term *kafir*. Thus, the seemingly contradictory concept of "*Kafir* among the People of the Book" (*kafir min ahl al-kitab*) in Islam should be understood to connote denial or disobedience of God's commands rather than unbelief in a theological sense.

The chief narrative function of the Qur'anic verses that apply the verb *kafara* to the Jews is to provide a rhetorical context for the rejection of the Prophet Muhammad's mission by the Jews of Arabia. For example, Qur'an 5:78 states: "Cursed were those among the Banu Isra'il who denied (*kafaru*) what was said by David and Jesus the Son of Mary. This was because they disobeyed and acted wantonly." This verse suggests that the rejection of the message of Islam by the Jews of Arabia was part of a long-standing tradition of disobedience and denial. With respect to the mission of Jesus the Qur'an states: "A group of the Banu Isra'il believed [in him] and a group disbelieved (*kafaru*)" (Qur'an 61:14). This verse implies that the Jews of Arabia who were true followers of the religion of Abraham should have followed the Prophet Muhammad just as a portion of the Banu Isra'il followed Jesus. However, the Jesus that is referred to in this verse is Jesus the Islamic Prophet, not Jesus Christ of Christianity.

The very limited application of the verb *kafara* to Jews in the Qur'an makes it abundantly clear that the prohibition of shared worship between Muslims and unbelievers in Qur'an 109 does not apply to Judaism in a theological sense. As stated earlier, the problem of the Jews from the Qur'anic perspective is disobedience rather than disbelief. However, a secondary issue that is also relevant to the creedal distinction between Islam and Judaism is the tendency of the Qur'an to combine the example of prophets like David and Moses, who are within the Jewish tradition, and prophets like Jesus and Muhammad, who are the founders of new religions. Rhetorically, this amalgamation of Jewish and non-Jewish prophets accentuates the distinctiveness of Islam with respect to Judaism. From the perspective of the Qur'an there is only one religion. Moses, David, Jesus, John the Baptist, and the other prophets mentioned in the Qur'an are all like the Islamic Abraham: they are neither Jews nor Christians but Muslims.

Historically, Muslims have construed the notion of Islam as a universal religion more as a theological limitation than as an opening for religious pluralism. For Muslim fideists the only way to truly worship Allah is to become Muslim. To prove their point they cite the following verse: "Verily the religion of God is Islam. Those who received the Book (i.e., Jews and Christians) differed only after knowledge came to them, through transgression among themselves. Those who deny the signs of God will find that God is quick in reckoning" (Qur'an 3:19). Contrary to this hegemonic position, however, there is another tradition of Islamic theology that sees Islam as expressed in the Qur'an as a primordial religion that goes beyond the creed historically associated with the Prophet Muhammad. This latter tradition provides a theological basis for arguing that Jews, Christians, and Muslims all worship the same God. As a theological doctrine it is close to Neusner's higher logic of monotheism: if there is only one religion, there can only be one God that monotheists worship.

It is possible to discern this higher logic in the following verse, which is one of the best-known creedal statements of monotheism in the Qur'an: "Your God is One God; there is no god but He, the Beneficent, the Merciful" (Qur'an 2:163). For medieval Sufis who speculated on the origin of religions this verse meant that all human beings, even polytheists, worship the One God Allah. However, those who are not creedally Muslim are unaware of the true nature of what they worship.[26]

In this regard it is important to point out that the word *Allah* is not a name. Although Muslims sometimes use *Allah* as if it were a name, the term is actually a contraction of the definite noun *al-ilah*, meaning "The God" or "The Divinity," as in the Greek phrase *ho theos*. In pre-Islamic Arabia, Allah was the Creator God, the God of the Heavens, and Lord of the Ka'ba in Mecca. This pre-Islamic concept of divinity is the subject of *Surat al-Ra'd* (Qur'an 13, "Lightning"), in which the Qur'an calls upon the Arabs to take the concept of Allah to its logical conclusion and recognize Him as the Only God: "Say: 'Allah is the creator of everything; He is the One, the Overwhelming'" (Qur'an 13:16). Historically, Islam did not introduce a completely new conception of God to the Arabian Peninsula. Instead, it used the well-known concept of Allah to eliminate all second-order divinities and powers. Islam brought Allah closer to human experience by stressing that The One God was both transcendent and immanently near:

> And when My servants question you concerning Me, verily
> I am near. I answer the prayer of the supplicant when he
> calls on Me. So let them heed my call and believe in Me, so
> that they might be guided rightly. (Qur'an 2:186)

According to the Jewish theologian Kaufmann Kohler, the concept of the religious creed was first introduced to Judaism under the influence of Islam.[27] Some of the earliest Jewish creeds came from Spain. For example the creed of Abraham Ben David Halevi (d. ca. 1180), who was born in Muslim Córdoba but died in Christian Toledo, sets forth six essentials of the Jewish faith: (1) the existence of God; (2) the unity of God; (3) the incorporeality of God; (4) the omnipotence of God; (5) the revelation and immutability of the Law; (6) divine Providence.[28] This and other early creeds were eventually overshadowed by the Thirteen Articles of Maimonides (d. 1204), which are still accepted by many Jews as a sort of semiofficial statement of Jewish theology. These Articles are as follows: (1) the existence of God; (2) the unity of God; (3) the spiritual nature of God; (4) the eternity of God; (5) the uniqueness of God as the sole object of worship; (6) belief in revelation through God's prophets; (7) the preeminence of Moses among the prophets; (8) belief in God's Law as given on Mount Sinai; (9) the immutability of the Torah as God's Law; (10) God's foreknowledge of men's actions; (11) belief in divine retribution; (12) belief in the Messiah; (13) belief in the resurrection of the dead.[29]

Although Kohler claims that Maimonides composed a creed that "formed a vigorous opposition to the Christian and Mohammedan creeds,"[30] only the preeminence of Moses among the prophets, the notion of the Torah as the final testament of God's Law, and the doctrine of the expected Messiah contradict the basic principles of Islam. According to the Qur'an, the Messiah is Jesus, the Qur'an confirms but replaces the Torah as the final testament, and the Prophet Muhammad confirms but replaces Moses as the preeminent prophet. However, Moses is arguably the most important prophet after Muhammad in Islam because he appears in the Qur'an more often than any other prophet including Muhammad, who is referred to by name only three times. Most important, none of the theological principles mentioned by Abraham Ben David or Maimonides contradicts the Islamic conception of God. On this basis it is possible to confirm that the God of Islam and the God of Israel are essentially the same; or more precisely, the God of Islam and the God of Rabbinic Judaism are the same.

However, as Jacob Neusner reminds us, the assertion that the God of Islam and the God of Israel is one can only come from a modern and comparative theological perspective. Muslim and Jewish fideists would both find it difficult to accept that the God of Islam and the God of Israel are the same. In the first place, the conflict over Israel and the status of Palestine has anathematized the term "Israel" to such an extent that few Muslims would want to associate with it, even theologically. Similarly, nowadays few Jews would want to associate with Islam. Another, more theological problem is that the concept of God has been personalized and particularized in both Islam and Judaism. As Neusner illustrates in his essay, the exclusivity of the traditional perspective on religion rules out sharing theological credit for monotheism with other communities of faith. Islamic theology is ignored in most works of Jewish theology. Islamic philosophers are mentioned from time to time only because of their influence on medieval Jewish theologians. Even Kaufmann Kohler, a theologian of Conservative Judaism who considers Christianity and Islam "daughter religions" of Judaism, fails to make a meaningful theological distinction between Christianity and Islam. In the book *Jewish Theology* he states, "The Church and the Mosque achieved great things in propagating the truths of the Sinaitic revelation among the nations, but added to it no new truths of an essential nature. Indeed, they rather obscured the doctrines of God's unity and holiness."[31] Whatever other differences might exist between Judaism and Islam, it is hard to see how any unbiased observer could say that Islam obscured the doctrines of God's unity and holiness.

However, in ignoring the numerous theological similarities between Judaism and Islam, Muslims are no different from Jews. For Muslims the sense of spiritual and moral exclusivity is reinforced by Qur'anic verses such as the following, which is often used in Friday sermons:

> You are the best community to emerge out of humankind: you enjoin morality, you forbid immorality, and you believe in Allah. If the People of the Book had believed it would have been better for them. Some of them are believers but most of them are transgressors. (Qur'an 3:110)

By stating that Muslims are "the best community to emerge out of humankind," the Qur'an reinforces the notion of Islamic exceptionalism and conditions Muslims to view the People of the Book as inferior, despite the theological similarities between Islam and Judaism.

The marginalization of the People of the Book is exacerbated by a quasi-Existentialist relation between the denial of God's commands and theological unbelief. This notion of denial is the "flipside" of the important Islamic concept of vicegerency (*al-khilafa*), by which the human being acts as God's representative and takes upon herself responsibility for the world. According to the logic of vicegerency, the person who rejects the commands of God abdicates her responsibility as a vicegerent and hence her moral reason for existence. This is illustrated by the following Qur'anic verse:

> It is [God] who made you vicegerents on Earth (*khala'ifa fi-l-ard*). If one rejects [God's command] the consequences of his unbelief are upon him (*fa man kafara fa-'alayhi kufruhu*); the unbelief of those who deny God only increases their abhorrence to the Lord. Truly the denial of the unbelievers only adds to their despair. (Qur'an 35:36)[32]

Although it is clear from the context of this verse that it was meant to refer to polytheists, the Existentialist message of "You are what you do," also allows it to be applied to Jews and Christians, and even to backsliding Muslims. Medieval Muslim polemics such as the "dialogue" between Ibn Lubb and the Jew discussed above illustrate that the rhetoric of disobedience and denial by which the Qur'an depicts the Jews helped foster the notion that disobedience of God was an inherent Jewish trait. If all human beings bear the responsibility of vicegerency, then how much greater is the responsibility of the Banu Isra'il, who were the original bearers of God's Covenant?

According to some verses of the Qur'an, the Prophets David and Jesus cursed the Banu Isra'il for disobedience so great that it attained the level of theological unbelief (Qur'an 5:78). Because of this in the Muslim popular imagination the disobedience of God by the Jews was forever "upon them" as a character trait. Historically, the notion of inherent Jewish disobedience became a self-fulfilling prophecy for

Muslims. For anti-Jewish polemicists, the proof of this in the Prophet Muhammad's time was that many Jews turned in friendship toward the pagans of Mecca instead of toward the Muslims, who should have been their natural allies. The Qur'an asks rhetorically of such people: "What reason do we (i.e., the Jews of Arabia) have *not* to believe in God and what has come to us of the Truth, and to hope that our Lord would admit us into the company of the righteous?" (Qur'an 5:84). Many Muslims would say today that if inconstancy and disobedience are natural characteristics of the Jews, how could anyone claim that Muslims and Jews worship the same God?

However, despite such arguments, only the blindest type of fideism and the most prejudiced form of sectarianism could obscure the theological compatibility between Judaism and Islam. The persistent attempts by Jews and Muslims to ignore each other throughout history is rendered even more unreasonable when one adds the similarity of the moral and ethical doctrines of Judaism and Islam to their theological compatibility. By prohibiting idolatry, murder, theft, sexual immorality, blasphemy, eating the flesh of an animal that is still alive, and establishing courts of law, Muslims can claim to abide by the seven Noahide Commandments of Judaism. By requiring the circumcision of males and establishing the Morning Prayer, Muslims can also claim to abide by the Jewish Commandments of Abraham. Finally, when one adds to this the lack of a formal priesthood, which Islam also shares with Rabbinic Judaism, it is hard not to be reminded of the famous biblical passage of Exodus 19:6, which states: "You shall be unto Me a kingdom of priests and a holy nation." Given the full extent of the theological and ethical similarities between Islam and Judaism, Qur'anic verses such as Qur'an 2:136, "[We believe in] what was revealed to Abraham, Isaac, Jacob, and the Tribes, and that which was given to Moses and Jesus and all of the Prophets from their Lord," cannot easily be dismissed as just rhetoric. It is clear that the Qur'anic vision of Islam encompasses not only the God of Abraham but much of the Jewish spiritual tradition as well.

Do Muslims and Christians Worship the Same God?

Although Islam is historically the last of the three Abrahamic religions to appear on the stage of world history, in many ways the discourse of the Qur'an places Islam in a medial position between Judaism and Christianity. With respect to its nomocentrism, or focus on law and ethics, Islam more closely resembles Judaism. Although Islam presents itself as the continuation of the religion of Abraham, Moses is a more apt model for the Prophet Muhammad than Abraham or any other prophet. Also as noted above, the tradition of law and ethics associated with the Jewish prophets is a prominent theme of Qur'anic discourse. However, the message of the Qur'an is also logocentric, or focused on the Word of God. Although Judaism also has a logocentric aspect and God spoke His Word directly to Moses (Qur'an 4:164), Jesus in the Qur'an embodies the Word of God (Qur'an 4:171) in a way that is more similar to (but not identical with) the Christian concept of the Logos. Islam is also more similar to Christianity in its missionary impulse and universalistic aspirations.

However, the Qur'an goes beyond both Judaism and Christianity by stating, "Every nation has a Messenger (*rasul*)" (Qur'an 10:47). Among Christian sects only Mormonism comes close to making such a claim for the universality of revelation. This implies that God's prophets are not limited to the Middle East and even may not be limited to the Abrahamic tradition. It is also why some Muslims have tried to include figures such as Krishna or the Buddha in the company of Islamic prophets. According to Kaufmann Kohler, Islamic universalism played a major role in influencing the Jews to consider their own version of monotheism as universal. In his opinion, the Jewish doctrine of divine unity "received special encouragement from the example of the leaders of Islam, whose victorious march over the globe was a triumph for the one God of Abraham over the triune God of Christianity."[33]

The Qur'an also stands theologically in a medial position between Judaism and Christianity, looking first at one tradition and then at the other when discussing the attributes of God. Most often the Qur'anic discourse on God is strongly reminiscent of Jewish monotheism, as in the verses of Qur'an 19:22-3:

> He is Allah, there is no other god but He; Knower of the unseen and the seen, He is the Merciful, the Compassionate. He is Allah, there is no other god but He; Possessor of All, the Holy, the Source of Safety, the Keeper of Faith, the Vigilant, the Glorious, the Irresistible, the Most Supreme; Exalted is He beyond what they associate with Him.

Verses like these are reminiscent of the Hebrew Bible's Book of Isaiah, such as when the God of Israel addresses the king of Persia:

> I am the Lord and there is none else; beside Me there is no God. I will gird thee, though thou dost not know Me, in order that the people shall know from the rising of the sun and from the west that there is none beside Me. I form the light and create the darkness; I make peace and also create evil, I am the Lord that doeth these things. (Isa. 45:5-7)[34]

By contrast, when the Qur'an turns toward Christianity, it draws sharper and more critical distinctions between the Islamic and Christian concepts of God. We have already seen how the Qur'an rejects the concept of the Trinity: "Those who say, 'Verily God is a third of three,' have denied the truth, for there is no God but one God" (Qur'an 5:73). Similarly, the Qur'an also rejects literalistic doctrines of Christology: "Those who say that God is the Messiah (*al-Masih*) Son of Mary deny the truth" (Qur'an 5:72). Verses such as these make it clear that when it comes to the concept of divine unity, the Qur'an seeks to draw a distinct line in the sand between Islamic and Christian definitions of monotheism. This can even be seen in verses that do not explicitly refer to Christianity. An important example of this can be found in *Surat al-Ikhlas* ("Sincere Faith"), which Muslims consider the definitive creedal statement of Qur'anic monotheism:

> Say: He is God the Only,
> God, the Perfect beyond compare.

He gives not birth, nor is He begotten,
And He is not, in Himself, dependent on anything. (Qur'an 112)

This Sura not only affirms the oneness of God but it also affirms that God is the Absolute: He is both incomparable and not contingent on anything. But this is not all. The Sura also contains an implicit refutation of the Nicene Creed of Christianity, which was formulated at the First Council of Nicaea in 325. This creed states that Jesus Christ is begotten of the Father and is the Father's "only begotten" (Gr. *monogenes*) son.[35] American Christians who are not scholars are often unaware that "begotten" means "born" and that the phrase "begotten not made" in the English version of the Nicene Creed means "born not created." Thus, when Qur'an 112 states that God "gives not birth nor is He begotten," it expresses the same notion of "begotten" or "born" as in the original Greek of the Nicene Creed. Theologically what this means is that in Islam, God should be considered neither Father nor Son.

In this respect it is also important to point out that when Jesus is referred to in the Qur'an he is called *'Isa*, his personal name in Arabic, or "The Messiah Son of Mary" (*al-Masih ibn Maryam*). *Christos*, the original Greek term for "Christ," is a loose translation of the Hebrew title *Mashiach* (Messiah), which means "The Anointed." Thus, just as with the concept of "begotten," the Qur'an's use of the title *al-Masih* for Jesus is in agreement with the language of early Christianity. It agrees with both the original Greek meaning of *Christos* and the Hebrew meaning of *Mashiach*. This represents another example of the Qur'an situating itself discursively between Judaism and Christianity. Although the Qur'an rejects the Christian assertion that Jesus is the Son of God, it agrees with Christianity against Judaism by affirming that the expected Christ or Messiah has already come and that his name was Jesus.

What does this mean for the question of whether Muslims and Christians worship the same God? The fact that the Qur'an takes a medial position between Judaism and Christianity would seem to

115

argue for an answer in the affirmative. On the other hand, the Qur'an's denial of the Trinity cannot be ignored. Furthermore, verses such as Qur'an 5:73 that deny the doctrine of Christology state categorically that those who believe that Jesus is God deny the Truth (*laqad kafara*). This denial is not a matter of disobedience or Covenant-breaking as with the Jews. These verses make it clear that the problem with Christology is theological. In addition, in order to emphasize Islam's rejection of the Trinity and Christology even more firmly, verse 5:73 ends with the following warning: "If they do not cease what they say, then those who are unbelievers among them will experience a grievous punishment."

Despite this warning, a trace of optimism can still be found in this verse. The phrase, "those who are unbelievers among them," implies that at least some Christians believe in ways that are theologically acceptable to Islam. But who are these believing Christians and what do they believe? Just as with the Jews, the Qur'an divides Christians as People of the Book into believers who are destined for salvation and deniers who are destined for the Fire. From their description in the Qur'an it appears that the People of the Book that God most admires are those who organize themselves into pious communities of worshipers:

> The People of the Book are not all alike. Among them is a community (*umma*) that stands reciting the verses of God throughout the night and bows down to Him in adoration. They believe in God and the Last Day; they enjoin good and forbid evil and hasten to do good works. These are among the righteous. Of the good that they do nothing will be rejected; for God is aware of those who revere Him. (Qur'an 3:113-15)

In addition to verses like these, the Qur'an also does not explicitly state that Christians are polytheists (*mushrikun*), as its rejection of the Trinity might imply. The tendency of medieval Muslim scholars to associate Christianity with polytheism came from later traditions and exegetical works. The closest that the Qur'an itself comes to associating Christianity with polytheism is to suggest guilt by rhetorical association. In Qur'an 5:72 Jesus the Messiah says to the Jews: "Oh Banu Isra'il! I worship Allah, my Lord and your Lord. If anyone joins partners with God, God will forbid heaven to him and his abode will be the Fire." Although this verse does not specify whether those who associate partners with God are Christians or polytheists, the fact that Jesus himself condemns those who associate partners with God seems to suggest that Christians who associate partners with God are like the polytheists. A similar rhetorical device can be seen in a prayer from the Qur'an that is often found in Sufi invocations: "Praise be to God, who never had a son, who never had a partner in His dominion, and who needs no ally to protect him from humiliation. So magnify Him greatly." (Qur'an 17:111) Here the Christian concept of the Son of God is linked with the concept of partnership, an association suggesting that if Trinitarianism is not polytheism, then at least it is not true monotheism.

The question of whether Muslims and Christians worship the same God is complicated further by apparent disagreements within Christianity itself over the object of Christian worship. Most Christian theologians agree that Jesus did not explicitly say, "I am God." However, the New Testament contains statements by Jesus and his disciples that suggest a greater than human status.[36] In evangelical Christianity, the doctrine of the divinity of Christ is a fundamental principle of the faith. In the widely respected textbook *Christian Theology*, the evangelical Baptist theologian Millard J. Erickson[37] cites four key theological implications of this doctrine:

1. The deity of Christ (this is Erickson's term) is crucial for the attainment of the knowledge of God. "Whereas the prophets came bearing a message from God, Jesus was God. If we would know what the love of God, the holiness of God, the power of God are like, we need only look at Christ."

2. The deity of Christ is crucial for the Christian concept of the redemption of sin. "It was not merely a finite human, but an

infinite God who died. He, the Life, the Giver and Sustainer of Life, who did not have to die, died."

3. God and humanity are reunited in the person of Christ. "It was not an angel or a human who came from God to the human race, but God himself crossed the chasm created by sin."

4. "Worship of Christ is appropriate. He is not merely the highest of the creatures, but he is God in the same sense and to the same degree as the Father. He is as deserving of our praise, adoration, and obedience as is the Father."[38]

If one compares the Qur'an's rejection of Christology with Erickson's notion of the deity of Christ, the line in the sand between Islam and Christianity appears as deep as a chasm. If this constitutes mainline Christianity, then the difference between Islam and Christianity with respect to the identity of Jesus Christ is theologically unbridgeable. According to Erickson, in evangelical theology Christ is not only divine but is coequal with the Father. He does not even admit a difference of attributes: "He is God in the same sense and to the same degree as the Father." He also states: "It was not merely a finite human, but an infinite God who died. He, the Life, the Giver and Sustainer of Life, who did not have to die, died."

From the perspective of Islamic theology, this last statement is not only bold but it would also be considered disrespectful of God. A Muslim would ask, "How could the God of Life, the Giver and Sustainer of Life, ever be said to die, even metaphorically?" If Erickson's notion of Christology were indeed fundamental Christian doctrine, then I would have to agree with conservative Christian leaders such as Pat Robertson who claim that Muslims and Christians do not worship the same God. If the Father and the Son are coequal, there is no way that a Muslim could agree with such a concept and creedally remain a Muslim. Many Christian writers have criticized the contention in Qur'an 5:72 that Christians believe "God is the Messiah Son of Mary," saying that it distorts the actual doctrines of Christology and the Trinity. However, Erickson's evangelical Christology seems to confirm this verse. If this is in fact what evangelical Christians believe, then from an Islamic point of view their *kufr* or denial of the Qur'anic doctrine of the humanity of Jesus Christ is both theological and creedally essential. One could only conclude that conservative evangelical theology draws the sharpest possible distinction between its notion of Christ-as-God and the God of Abraham as conceived by Islam and by Judaism as well.

Fortunately for the sake of the Ethiopian's Dilemma, conservative evangelical Christology is not the only version of Christology in contemporary Christianity. A surprising aspect of Erickson's summary of Christology is that the Holy Spirit, the third person of the Trinity, is not mentioned. From the outside his image of the divine Christ as God come to earth resembles a Hindu avatar. By being coequal with the Father, the human persona of Christ seems completely subsumed by the divine persona. The Holy Spirit does not appear at all in this formulation. In recent decades, some Methodist and Anglican theologians have become concerned about the absence of a fully Trinitarian perspective in Christian worship. A recent survey conducted by Asbury Theological Seminary (a Wesleyan seminary located in Kentucky) found that of the seventy-two favorite hymns used in Christian services between1989 and 2004, none explicitly referred to the Trinity or the triune nature of God and only three songs named all three persons of the Trinity.[39] The Methodist theologian Geoffrey Wainwright argued in his 1984 book *Doxology* that the only way that Christian worship could make sense was to conceive of it from a strictly Trinitarian perspective.[40] For Wainwright, Christians worship the Father through the Son in the Holy Spirit. The late Edinburgh theologian James B. Torrance, a student of Karl Barth, makes a similar argument in the 1997 *Worship, Community, and the Triune God of Grace*.[41] For Torrance, the primary object of Christian worship is God the Father; worship is mediated by Christ and enabled by the Holy Spirit. He further defines worship as "the gift of participating through the Spirit in the incarnate Son's communion with the Father."[42] Either of these perspectives, but especially Wainwright's, is more compatible with Islamic theology than evangelical Christology as defined by Millard J. Erickson. Although the Trinity remains a contested concept and the notion of Christ's Incarnation is also rejected in Islam, at least in the Christological formulations of Wainwright and Torrance, a meaningful distinction is made between the different persons of the Trinity.

Torrance begins his book by asking the question, "Who do Christians worship?" This is also an important question to ask when determining whether Christians and Muslims worship the same God. If the object of worship is a fully divine Jesus Christ as in Erickson's formulation, then there really is nothing to talk about. Muslims worship God the Absolute: God the Only (*al-Ahad*), God the Incomparable (*al-Samad*), God the Transcendent beyond all form and comparison, as in the words of *Surat al-Ikhlas*. According to Erickson, this is not what evangelical Christians worship. Therefore, the only conclusion to draw is that Muslims and evangelical Christians do not worship the same God. However, if as Methodist theologian Geoffrey Wainwright says, Christians worship the Father through the Son in the Holy Spirit, there is still something to talk about between Christians and Muslims. Although the Incarnation and deity of Christ are rejected in Islam, it is at least possible to argue that worshiping God the Father is something like worshiping God the Absolute. It is still not possible to bridge the theological differences between Islam and Christianity enough to create some kind of Abrahamic World Theology, but a strictly Trinitarian theology of worship can at least provide some common ground.

The concepts of the Father and the Son as conceived theologically in Christianity do not exist in Islam. Qur'an 9:30 states: "The Jews (*al-yahud*) call 'Uzayr (Ezra) the son of God and the Christians call the Messiah the Son of Mary the Son of God. This is only a figure of speech (literally, 'words from their mouths') that they copied from what previous deniers of the Truth used to say." The Qur'an even criticizes the metaphorical use of the term "son of God." Qur'an 5:18 criticizes both Jews and Christians who say, "We are the sons of God and are beloved of Him." The problem with this usage is both theological and moral. Theologically, the Qur'an is insistent about avoiding any-thing—even a figure of speech—that might complicate the simplicity of pure monotheism. Morally, the Qur'an is also concerned with dispelling the notion that a particular people are so beloved of God that they are assured of salvation or are beyond moral reproach. From the Qur'an's perspective such a sense of entitlement might lead to serious moral injustices. A person who feels assured of forgiveness to an irrational degree is liable to commit any injustice with impunity. The answer of the Qur'an to the conceit of spiritual entitlement is to say: "Then why has [God] punished you for your sins? Nay, you are but ordinary human beings that He has created. He forgives whom He chooses and He punishes whom He chooses" (Qur'an 5:18).

Unlike the concepts of the Father and the Son, the concepts of the Logos and the Holy Spirit do exist in the Qur'an but in a way that is different from Christianity. In the Qur'an Jesus and his mother Mary are called signs (*ayat*) of God (Qur'an 23:51) and Jesus is called a sign (*'alam*) of the Day of Judgment (Qur'an 43:61). The Qur'an also states: "The Messiah Jesus Son of Mary was a Messenger of God and His Word (*kalima*) and Spirit (*ruh*), which [God] bestowed on Mary" (Qur'an 4:171). According to the Qur'an, the Word of God or Logos is embodied in Jesus; this plus his virgin birth make him unique among God's Messengers. He is different from other Messengers, however, only in bearing the Logos personally. In this, he is equivalent not to God, but to the *Injil* (the Evangel or Gospel), the Book of Wisdom that was derived from his teachings. The second part of Qur'an 4:171 states: "So believe in God and His Messengers but do not say 'Three' (i.e., the Trinity), for desisting is better for you. Verily, God is One God. Exalted is He above having a son!" The uniqueness of Jesus Christ by virtue of his virgin birth does not make him divine either. By being created in the Spirit and nurtured in Mary's womb he was like Adam the first human being, who was also created from God's Spirit but molded out of earth: "The similitude of Jesus with respect to God is like that of Adam: [God] created him from earth and said to him, 'Be!' And he was" (Qur'an 3:59).

In the Qur'an the Holy Spirit (*al-Ruh al-Qudus*, like the Hebrew *Ruach ha-Kodesh*) is sometimes associated with Jesus and is sometimes independent of him. The most important verse that associates Jesus with the Holy Spirit is Qur'an 5:110, a lengthy verse that deserves to be reproduced in full:

> Behold! God will say: "O Jesus Son of Mary! Recall My blessings on you and your mother. Behold! I strengthened you with the Holy Spirit, so that you could speak to people in childhood and in maturity. Behold! I taught you the Book (*al-kitab*) and the Wisdom (*al-hikma*): the Torah and the Gospel. Behold! You made the figure of a bird out of clay by My permission, and then you breathed into it and it became a bird by My permission, and you healed the blind and the lepers by My permission. Behold! You bring forth the dead by My permission. Behold! I restrained the Banu Isra'il from [harming] you when you showed them the clear signs, and the deniers of the Truth among them said: 'This is nothing but apparent magic.'"

This verse illustrates the two ways in which the Qur'an discusses the concept of the Spirit. First, the Holy Spirit is used by God to provide guidance and inspiration to the Prophets and the believers. This can be seen in the passage, "I strengthened you with the Holy Spirit, so that you could speak to people in childhood and maturity." Second, a more general concept of the Spirit also appears in the Qur'an. This unmodified concept of Spirit (*al-Ruh*) refers to the breath of life or the divine quickening that animates our human spirits. It is often overlooked that this Spirit also has a divine origin. The Qur'an advises the Prophet Muhammad: "They ask you about the Spirit (*al-Ruh*). Say: 'The Spirit is from the command (*amr*) of My Lord, but only a little of its knowledge has been revealed to you'" (Qur'an 17:85). Jesus is called the "Spirit of God" (*Ruh Allah*) in Islam because both types of Spirit were within him. The Holy Spirit as a source of revelation resulted in the miracle of the *Injil*, the book of Christ's wisdom teachings transmitted by his disciples. In this he was like every other Messenger in Islam, including the Prophet Muhammad. What makes Jesus Christ different from other Messengers is that in his person the Holy Spirit was combined with the quickening Spirit, which enabled him to perform his most noteworthy miracles, such as reviving the dead and bringing life to a bird made of clay.

However, in Islamic theology the indwelling of the Spirit does not make Jesus Christ divine; instead, he represents the highest realization of Adamic humanity. All of his miracles came from a source outside of himself: "By [God's] permission," as the Qur'an says. Thus, the difference between Jesus and Adam is one of degree but not of substance. The Spirit dwelt in Adam as well. One implication of the Qur'anic critique of Christianity is that the deification of a single man in the person of Christ amounts to selling short the full potential of the human being. From an Islamic point of view, the Christian doctrine of the imitation of Christ (*imitatio christi*) would make better sense if Christ were fully human. To be fully imitable he would have to be a man: a perfected man perhaps, but still a man. The Qur'an rarely misses a chance to remind its readers that because Adam is the father of all humanity his potential is our potential. As the Second Adam, the same can be said of Jesus Christ. If God wills, his potential can be our potential too. This essential concept of Islamic humanism is expressed in Qur'an 15:28-29: "Behold! Your Lord said to the angels: 'I am about to create a human being from a lump of molded earth. When I have fashioned him and breathed a portion of My Spirit into him, bow down to him in prostration.'"

Conclusion: From Comparison to Counterpoint

Do Jews, Christians, and Muslims worship the same God? Based on the preceding discussion the short answer to this question from the Islamic perspective is yes with respect to Jews and maybe or it depends with respect to Christians. However, if Millard J. Erickson's interpretation of Christology is an accurate representation of evangelical theology, then the answer would have to be no with respect to evangelical Christians. As stated above, there is no way to make Erickson's assertion that Jesus Christ is God "in the same sense and to the same degree as the

Father" theologically acceptable in Islam. The Qur'an is very explicit on this point: Christians who literally believe that Jesus the Son of Mary is God are theologically unbelievers who do not worship the same God as Muslims do. However, with respect to more strictly Trinitarian Christians like the Methodist theologian Geoffrey Wainwright, who advocates worshiping the Father through the Son in the Holy Spirit, it is possible—although still problematic—to argue that Christians and Muslims worship the same God. This is because common ground between Christian and Islamic theology can be found in the concept of God the Father. God the Father in Trinitarian theology shares many of the attributes of God in the Qur'an. Thus, when engaging in inter-religious dialogue with Christians, Muslims could avoid the theological problem of the Son by focusing on the Father and the Holy Spirit.

Another conclusion that is much easier to draw from a comparison of Islamic and Jewish theology is how silly it is for Muslims and Jews to treat each other with the kind of enmity that exists today. Theologically there are few significant differences between the God of Islam and the God of Judaism. Muslims and Jews both worship a God of Abraham that is to all intents and purposes the same. Although second-order theological differences do exist, such as the acceptance of secondary powers in premodern Rabbinic Judaism and the strongly gendered language (both male and female) that is used for divinity in Kabbalah, these can be explained as owing to historical and cultural factors or the use of specialized forms of rhetoric. Many contemporary Jewish theologians already take this approach. For example, the Conservative Jewish theologian Kaufmann Kohler used a combination of cultural-evolutionary and psychological arguments to explain such doctrines. A Muslim could do the same and still remain true to the creedal boundaries of Islam.

From a critical theological perspective, I would argue that what has kept Jews and Muslims from seeing each other as natural allies is the question of ownership. This problem manifests itself on a number of different levels. Ownership issues that are currently contested between Jews and Muslims include the ownership of land, the ownership of genealogical precedence, the ownership of historical precedence, the ownership of moral leadership, the ownership of political authority, the ownership of religious authenticity, the ownership of doctrinal purity, and finally and perhaps most importantly, the ownership of God. Jacob Neusner's essay in this volume is an important reminder of the crucial role that the ownership of God has played in traditional Jewish responses to Islam. One can imagine how shocking it must have been for premodern Jews to see the descendants of Ishmael take the God of Israel away from Israel and give Him to the entire world in the name of Islam. However, herein lies the problem. If Muslims had been more attentive to the theology of the Qur'an than to their imperialist or triumphalist inclinations, they might have realized that God was not theirs to give. Nor was God Israel's to possess. Qur'an 2:156 states: "We belong to God and to Him is the return." God does not belong to anyone. Rather, we belong to Him. Anglican Bishop Kenneth Cragg expressed this theological truism both profoundly and succinctly at the closing session of the first Building Bridges conference of Muslim and Christian scholars at Lambeth Palace in London in 2002. When asked what was his advice for the promotion of Christian-Muslim understanding, he replied, "God is not a predicate."[43] This advice is just as important for Muslim-Jewish relations as it is for Muslim-Christian relations.

Although resolving the Ethiopian's Dilemma remains difficult for Muslims and Jews, it is even harder to resolve for Muslims and Christians because of the greater theological distance between Islam and Christianity. Despite my suggestion that in dialogues with Christians, Muslims could avoid theological disputes over the Trinity by focusing on the Father and the Holy Spirit, this does not solve the Ethiopian's Dilemma. Avoiding this issue merely sidesteps the theological problem of the identity of Christ. In a recent review of Miroslav Volf's book, *Allah: A Christian Response*,[44] Gavin D'Costa attempted to clarify the question of whether Christians and Muslims worship the same God by posing two additional questions: "God" at what stage and "God according to whom?"[45] In this essay I tried to make the same point by drawing a distinction between Millard J. Erickson's description of conservative evangelical Christology and the Trinitarian Christologies of Geoffrey Wainwright and James B. Torrance. Based on this analysis, the most accurate answer to the question of whether Christians worship the same God as Muslims would be, "It depends on their Christology." Surprisingly, I have yet to see a Christian response to this question—including Miroslav Volf's—that makes systematic comparisons between different types of Christology. Instead, most Christian responses tend to fall back (as Volf's does) on a prefabricated notion of "orthodox" Trinitarianism that combines the three persons of the Trinity into a single monistic unity.[46] However, as a Muslim scholar looking at Christology from the outside, I would submit that Millard J. Erickson's version of Christology does not conform to this model of Trinitarianism. Does this mean that Christological differences are more apparent than real or does it mean that Erickson's evangelical Christology is not "orthodox" Christianity?

I would suspect that in an unguarded moment Miroslav Volf would say that Erickson's Christology is not orthodox. In his book he cites Archbishop of Canterbury Rowan Williams's formulation of a threefold pattern of interdependent action within a single divine nature as representative of Trinitarian orthodoxy.[47] In fact, the notion of the Trinity as "one single and undivided divine essence" is crucial to Volf's definition of Christian monotheism.[48] Nowhere in his book does he address different versions of Christology—in fact, he hardly addresses the subject of Christology at all. But doesn't this approach beg the question of different approaches to Christology in contemporary Christianity? Apart from the conservative evangelical example, what about Seventh Day Adventist Christology? What about Jehovah's Witnesses Christology? What about Christian Science Christology? What about Latter-day Saints Christology? The list can go on and on. Rather than avoiding such issues, in my opinion we could all learn more if we took the more difficult intellectual road rather than the easier one.

Ecumenism is not necessarily a good thing if it causes us to avoid important issues. On the other hand, it is also considered foolish to hang out one's dirty linen where one's rivals can see it. In 1704 Daniel Defoe wrote in *Dictionarium Sacrum Seu Religiosum* that in treating the matter of differences within Christianity it was important to avoid "using the Opprobrious Names of Schismaticks or Sectaries and the like Appellations, which serve to rend them asunder, instead of cementing them together against the *Common Enemy*."[49] Today, more than three hundred years later, ecumenism within Judaism, Christianity, and Islam still serves to hinder ecumenism across the Abrahamic religions. A comparative theological project such as the one we are engaged in requires both courage and mutual trust. To struggle honestly with the question of whether Jews, Christians, and Muslims worship the same God requires a theology that is not only comparative but self-critical as well.

For too long Islam has been treated as an upstart in theological dis-cussions among scholars of the Abrahamic religions. To a certain extent this is to be expected because as the "newest" of the Abrahamic reli-gions, Islam is often regarded by Jews and Christians as a party crasher. However, Islam's status as a historical latecomer also gives it a unique perspective from which to assess both Judaism and Christianity theo-logically. An example of this can be seen in the preceding discussion of Christology. By approaching the issue of Christology from the outside, an Islamic perspective can highlight theological differences that may have been ignored. In the 2007 *Statistical Abstract of the United States*, evangelical Christians made up 28.6 percent of the US population. By contrast, 24.5 percent were Catholics and only 13.9 percent were mainline Protestants. It is hard to dispute the fact that today evangelical Christians are more numerous and hence demographically just as "main-line" as mainline Protestants. Because of this fact their theology can no longer be ignored but has to be taken seriously. An honest, self-critical and comparative theological discussion of Christology that includes Jews, Muslims, and different varieties of Christians could take an impor-tant step in this direction and be beneficial to Christianity itself.

In writing this essay I tried to conduct a serious investigation of the theological similarities and differences between Islam, Judaism, and Christianity and to see what light this shed on the question of whether Jews, Christians, and Muslims worship the same God. In this process my research turned up what seemed to be a theological discrepancy between evangelical Christology (Erickson) on the one hand and mainline Protestant (Wainwright and Torrance) and perhaps also Catholic (Volf) Christology on the other. However, I am no expert on Christology. The discrepancy that I saw with Muslim eyes may be more apparent than real. It would help me as a Muslim scholar to understand more about Christianity if the discussion begun here could be taken further. Similarly critical but respectful theological investigations of Islam by Jewish and Christian theologians might turn up comparable discrepancies between Sunni theology, Shiite theology, and Sufi theology. They might even discover that Salafi Sunni theology differs in significant ways from "mainline" (i.e., classical medieval) Sunni theology. In each of these cases the comparative perspective of an outsider would be useful in casting new light on one's own theological tradition.

The final conclusion of this essay is that with respect to the theological differences between Christianity and Islam, the Ethiopian's Dilemma is not likely to be resolved any time soon. In some ways the division between the two religions is even greater than it was in the time of Ellá Seham, the Negus of Abyssinia. But this does not have to be seen as a permanent impediment to Muslim-Christian understanding. It just might mean instead that we need new tools for our workshop. One approach that might be helpful would be to replace a comparative perspective on religious differences with a *contrapuntal* perspective. In the book *Culture and Imperialism*, Edward W. Said proposed the contrapuntal perspective as a way "to think through and interpret together experiences that are discrepant, each with its particular agenda and pace of development, its own internal formations, its internal coherence and system of external relationships, all of them coexisting and interacting with others."[50] It seems to me that this is also what we need to promote meaningful theological dialogues between Muslims, Christians, and Jews. The use of counterpoint is especially valuable, says Said, in the attempt "to make concurrent those views and experiences that are ideologically and culturally closed to each other and that attempt to distance or suppress other views and experiences."[51]

In effect, this is what I have tried to do in the previous pages. In the case of Islam and Judaism I tried to clarify a major theological agreement that had been obscured ideologically. In the case of Islam and Christianity I tried to highlight what I saw as the key theological difference between the two religions and in the process suggested that we should look further into the discrepancies that apparently exist within Christian theology itself. In neither case did I try to paper over existing differences or homogenize them in the name of an inauthentic world theology. Said proposed the contrapuntal approach as a means of starting a constructive dialogue on the basis of difference rather than similarity. I would add to this by asserting that this is the best way for Jews, Christians, and Muslims to engage in meaningful religious dialogue and still remain true to their creedal traditions. I would also suggest that this is what the Negus of Abyssinia did when he called the pagan Meccans and the Muslim refugees together to interrogate Islam. His concern was not to determine whether Islam was the same as Christianity, but to discern whether its differences from Christianity stayed within an acceptable range of dialogue according to his creed. This is why in his statements he focused on the source of Islam's teachings and the extent of its differences with respect to Christology. He too seems to have understood that it is not in comparison but in counterpoint where the greatest benefits of interreligious dialogue dwell.

Epilogue: But Even So, Look at That!

Martin E. Marty

Some readers will greet the conclusions, or nonconclusions, of the four scholars in this book with disappointment or disdain, as they have addressed the question, Do monotheist religions worship the same God? Whoever might bring hopes that a panel such as this could come up with easy answers to the question has to see such hopes dashed. The authors bring the proper credentials to the inquiry. They are at home with and can expound findings and proposals from theologians, historians, and textual scholars in the various religious and secular communities through the centuries. Some of them manifest hopes that they could formulate answers satisfying to scholars in such communities, but they all stop short of making the claim that they have succeeded.

Disdain will be the response of others who came to this book with sure answers to the question. Some of them may see the whole venture as futile, shelving this with other unanswerable questions such as, Why is there something and not nothing? Various textual and religious traditions do settle *that* question simply: by contending that God, *their* God in scriptures, *their* scriptures, settled it. These people might also have solved the issue philosophically or scientifically to their own satisfaction, whether or not they can peddle their answers widely and effectively. So it is with the question in this title, *Do Jews, Christians, and Muslims Worship the Same God?* From some the immediate answer is, *Of course* Jews, Christians, and Muslims do not worship the same God. The "other two" faith traditions besides one's own are false and should be dismissed out of hand. Raising our question is not tantalizing or worthwhile, because it is futile, obvious, and dishonest—the answer yes or no is evident before anyone can discuss and debate options.

If readers will not all be fully satisfied with emphatic answers to the question, why pose it in the first place? What use is it? What might be an outcome of further inquiry? My response, after reading these essays is similar to one that comes to mind when something goes wrong in any inquiry, including the scientific. I once posed this in a discussion of comparative utopian visions. Having pointed out that *all* utopian proposals, programs, and experiments have failed, and so assuming that they will all fail, we historians who study them had to ask why we had pursued them. The thoughtful physician-scientist Lewis Thomas provided a suggestion. Hearing too often that we learn through trial and error, he argued that we do not learn through error, but through what we do and think after the error has been made. The key moment after an experiment has gone wrong is when someone assesses the damages of the failure and then moves on, saying something like: "But even so, look at that!" In effect, "Behold!"—a common translation for the Greek word *theoria*, "theory."[1]

Those who judge, as I do, that there can be no fully authoritative answer to the question, Do monotheist religions worship the same God? have to justify both the effort we make in this book and to charter further dialogue among the faith communities. Unless a new universally accepted divine revelation appears, one that is capable of transcending and even abolishing the memory of those that have gone before, we are stuck with religious Scriptures whose implied answer will not be compelling among traditions that do not accept their claims to uniqueness in truth-claims.

Similarly, given the diversity of philosophical claims and answers within various competing traditions, it is not likely that we will see one set of them prevailing over all others. This is so even when one text or answer within a system is backed with authority, as in the case of totalitarian enforcements of their "truths." Note how Baruch Levine sets up the "even so" issue and responds in his first two lines:

Question: Do Jews, Christians, and Muslims all worship the same God?

Answer: Yes, of course, but . . .

A simple, bold, and frank yes would have elicited one kind of argument, which might have looked like a dead end to many readers. The same, however, would have been the case with a simple, bold, and frank no. Levine resists both easy responses, but holds us with his equivalent, "Even so, look at that!" Yes, of course, but . . .

Pages later, after having probed the case, he returns to his seemingly simple format with a complex answer:

So we ask: Who holds the rights to the one, true God?

Answer: All who worship him sincerely, as it is written: "The Lord is near to all his 'callers'; to all who call upon him truthfully." (Ps. 145:18)

He modifies the original question from, Who is our God? to, in his view, more properly, Who are God's people? The question is not, Is God on our side? but rather, Are we on God's? To which still other readers will add another Yes, but . . .

Continuing the Conversation to Practice Civility

Observe in all four chapters, the combination of agreements and disagreements, which makes the current dialogue both tantalizing and provocative. We might ask why these four authors or any similar combination of scholars could reasonably bid for our time and attention as they have done here. A first answer has to do with the civil tone and character. Ideas have consequences, and the idea that one's own tradition, communion, or tribe uniquely possesses truth can be dangerous. Sacred texts often include divinely revealed sanctions for the exclusion of others, an exclusion that throughout history—and perhaps never more so than today—legitimates killing the other, making war, seeking annihilation of other ideas, persons, and populations. Any dialogue that lays bare such claims and then challenges them, for example through religious studies that relativize the murderous claims of a particular tradition, and contributes to the prevention of genocide and the promotion of peace.

With all the good will in the world, the one who simply universalizes an answer cannot solve the problem with a yes. On occasion one hears a partner in dialogue who deplores religious conflict and then offers a resolution to this effect: "If we just talk the religions out of what they hold separately and have them affirm just one big declaration of faith in God, all will be well." All too often, vanity presses attract— what is now even more easily available in this era of self-published books—books with a broad but ungrounded answer. Some of these are designed on a cosmic scale as an answer to everything by defining a religion to which all could presumably agree and that will provide a base for moral discourse while bringing salvation to all. Previously such books were sold to a few friends of the author, if they could not wriggle free of the sales-pitching author's arms. Today, this type of book may attract a few "Like" on the Internet, but we don't have to like the superficialities.

Continuing the Conversation to Learn from Others

The authors in this book point out that comparative studies can also reveal *traditions and ideas from which others can learn,* even when they do not agree on the most dramatic point. People in one Abrahamic tradition may not have to regard another as the possessor of absolute truth about God in order to learn from elements in the witness and activity of another. Even to read how others have struggled with the question of whether the monotheist religious traditions worship the same God is an activity that can lead a reader to unfamiliar intellectual terrain, where a variety of growths dealing with questions can enhance one's understanding. So we do not, to the satisfaction of all, worship the same God? "Even so, look at that!" we may say as we deal with such growths. For example, I do not have to agree with the ultimate root of the theology associated with Tolstoy or Tutu or Saint Francis in order to profit from reading what they have to say about peace within their own contexts, while they go about promoting universal understandings. Am I ignorant or prejudiced if I do not respond when I hear "Even so, look at that!"? Perhaps, because I would stand no chance of seeing my own repertoire of options enlarged if I never heeded, never inquired, never conversed.

Intending to learn is to take seriously the narratives of other traditions, those having revelatory power. Philosophers and theologians who deal with "the whole" may be impatient with such provincial or "bounded" stories. But we all have to deal with the consequence that comes with the understanding, voiced by Alasdair MacIntyre, that humans are "story-telling animals."[2] These stories, at the heart of faiths, often complicate the concept of the One who is witnessed to. Bruce Chilton makes it sound direct enough:

> To assert God's sameness in the three Abrahamic religions may seem straightforward, following from God's oneness; some version of that claim is often heard. But exclusions of faith perspectives, both across theologies and within theological traditions, are considerable when the Abrahamic religions are privileged with this assumption.

He illustrates by dealing with the "privileged" faith perspective of Christians, focused as it is with the particular story of Jesus within the Godhead.

The stories may have universal significance, but finding the limits of the power of such myths or root narratives in another communion or community can bring realism to the efforts. This has been well proposed by philosopher George Santayana:

> Any attempt to speak without speaking any particular language is not more hopeless than the attempt to have a religion that shall be no religion in particular . . . thus every living and healthy religion has a marked idiosyncrasy. Its power consists in its special and surprising message and in the vistas which that revelation gives to life. The vistas it opens and the mysteries it propounds are another world to live in, and another world to live in—whether we expect ever to pass wholly over into it or no—is what we mean by having a religion.[3]

Santayana's words such as "message," "vista," and "mystery," within theistic religions, be they characterized as mono- or poly-, at heart are based in the concept of our witness to "God" or gods. Now, speaking of monotheism, whether or not this God is the "same" in the other traditions affects all other parts of the messages, vistas, and mysteries in each communion and must be reckoned with by all who want to deal constructively with their relations to one another.

Continuing the Conversation Is Difficult and Complex

Another of the values of chapters like those in this book results from the authors' general readiness to show how difficult and complex understanding of "the other" actually is. These authors deal with *difficulty and complexity* not to display scholarly credentials or to warn others off, as some scholars have done with subjects like these. Nor do they evidence that they want to keep the masses, the regular folks, at a distance from their scholarly preserve. Their point is to suggest that superficial engagement with these issues is not helpful. Participants in interfaith dialogues or in the efforts of pluralistic communities to find commonalities have often heard abrupt summaries such as, "Well, after all, we are all simply in different boats heading for the same shore." In religious inquiries, that "shore" does not necessarily mean only a "life to come" after each mortal dies, but includes everything important in the scope of religion.

If the God of one faith determines everything, the question of the fate of those who profess belief in and who follow another faith remains a demanding issue. If all such fates are determined without examination upfront, then all the other questions of morals, ethics, meaning, and purpose are unimportant. Thoughts about God's relation to believers and nonbelievers obviously do differ from community to community (and obviously also within communities), and the question who it is that they worship remains complex and troubling and has to be taken seriously by those in each community. Those who participate in interfaith dialogue may choose to do so only to try to convert others who disagree with them. Or they may want to use occasions of dialogue as instances where they can parade the virtues and boasts of their messages. But not all are arrogant or devious: some earnestly keep asking questions as to whether they are worshiping the same God for a variety of valid reasons.

Awareness Stimulates and Legitimates Conversation

Awareness of the complexity of what "the other" holds and professes *stimulates legitimates dialogue* or, less formally, conversation. The authors of this book write with an effort to make such conversation more meaningful, in the "Even so, look at that" spirit. While each might have been capable of engaging in argument all along, they will do so with a fresh understanding of its limits and proper place. Such conversation has always been difficult, since it deals with the self and the "other," in this case the other community or tradition. These four authors also show awareness of the urgency impelling dialogue today. This urgency has grown in our global society, whose members can frightfully contend over the question of God or the gods.

Recognizing How Strange We Are to One Another

It is hard to read the chapters in this book without coming to a new awareness of how strange strangers are to one another. Even the modes of discourse in the various communities are strange to the other. A lifetime in religious historical scholarship did not prepare me to feel acquainted with, for instance, Jacob Neusner's exposition of classical Judaism). The concept of "the minim," for example, had not reached me nor has it become familiar even under Neusner's patient guidance. So I join the company of those who were strangers. Georg Simmel described the situation of the stranger, which is so central to talk of "monotheistic religions."[4]

> The stranger . . . is fixed within a particular spatial group, or within a group whose boundaries are similar to spatial boundaries. But his position in this group is determined essentially by the fact that he has not belonged to it from the beginning, that he imports qualities into it, which do not and cannot stem from the group itself.

There are no higher values to a monotheist in any tradition than those associated with the God being worshiped within it, so boundaries become important.

A complex dialectic emerges in the cultures we call pluralistic and on a globe which is crowded with interactive peoples.

> The stranger is close to us, insofar as we feel between him and ourselves common features of a national, social, occupational [this author would also add "religious"], or generally human nature. He is far from us, insofar as these common features extend beyond him or us, and connect only because they connect a great many people.

Monotheists, in this argument or observation, are "close to each other," because they are all "theists," worshiping and witnessing to one God, and they are "far from us," because they belong to the company of a "great many people" with vastly differing and even contradictory claims. The authors in this book have been consistent in their observation that "God" is of ultimate concern in the three communities about which they generalize. Yes, being "close to us," and "our" community does not resolve everything, because "the great many people" who make up the Jewish, Christian, and Muslim "communities," internally divided as they are, have to deal with the issue of the boundaries of their witness and worship both among themselves and between "them" and "us."

"But even so, look at that!" as we must. A first accompaniment or issue of that look threatens to and often does lead to conflict, on occasion with murderous and annihilating intent. The fact that the other, the stranger, the apostate, the infidel with whom I compete, who may prosper and threaten me, still tempts me to make rigid defensible boundaries but it also limits me. Hence both the potential of increase in harmony across boundaries and also the increase of threat of disharmony turned murderous relate to the question of God but also the equally important and in fact prior question: Do we all worship a God, any God, let alone the same God?

This illustration is born of personal experience and it illustrates the complexity of lived approaches to the question of this book. In 1995, before a United Nations conference in Brussels on Women's Reproductive Rights, Family Planning, and Migration, a foundation subsidized another conference of scholars that I chaired. They were from, roughly, a score of nations and a dozen religious traditions. The conference's task was to debate controversial topics such as "birth control," "abortion," and "rights." Only one chair at the table was held by a religious community that had a seat in the United Nations, the Vatican. All the others represented nongovernmental organizations from elsewhere who, it was hoped, might have some influence at or creative interpretation of the UN Conference.

Though most were strangers to each other, they made progress toward a consensus statement, but necessarily fell short on the most controversial issues. The representative of Vatican interests kept arguing that there should be compensatory efforts at a consensus statement. "Couldn't we at least in a preamble state our common belief in God?" "No," said a Japanese Buddhist. "My tradition is as 'religious' as yours is, and we take 'life' as seriously as you do. But we do not believe in 'God.'" Pressed by the Catholic participant, he informally described something like the "holy emptiness" that some have adjudged to be central to Buddhism. He was effective at his representation, and consequently "God" disappeared from the reckoning of these informed and serious scholars of the various traditions. Here again, one had to point again and exclaim, "But, even so, look at that!" And the participants looked and made constructive comment on other features of the traditions in respect to the issues of the conference.

Something like this occurs in, for instance, numberless meetings in a pluralistic society like the United States. Intelligent, concerned, often passionate citizens make constructive statements and proposals. But if representatives of our nation's largest community, in this case the Christian, make grounding assumptions based only on Christian concepts of God, they are not going to win favor even among all their "Judeo-Christian" kin. Jews, for scores of years, have had to argue that being with Christians in communion with God through or, more definitely, *only* through Jesus Christ, is not tolerable. Add to that contention among monotheists the role and language of Islam, and it becomes clear that the "one God" as "one" and as "God" cannot be taken for granted and is likely to be rejected by many faithful people.

Through international conferences and a half century of experience with interfaith dialogue, informed by considerable reading of texts sacred to the tradition and modern research and writing on the subject, I have seen enough ancillary or corollary profit to motivate continuing efforts to find value in interfaith conversation, in studies to encourage others, and to learn from scholars like those who wrestle with a basic issue in this book.

Dialogue with the Character of Conversation

Critics charge that it is frivolous and fruitless for specialists with certain tastes, much time, and more patience to continue the conversation if they cannot agree on the main point. After all, if dialogue has the character of conversation that my colleague David Tracy outlined so well, will it be fulfilling and in any way practical?

> Conversation is a game with some hard rules: say only what you mean; say it as accurately as you can; listen to and respect what the other says, however different or other; be willing to correct or defend your opinions if challenged by the conversation partner; be willing to argue if necessary, to confront if demanded, to endure necessary conflict, to change your mind if the evidence suggests it. These are merely some generic rules for questioning. As good rules, they are worth keeping in mind n case the questioning does begin to break down. In a sense they are merely variations of the transcendental imperative elegantly articulated by Bernard Lonergan. "Be attentive, be intelligent, be responsible, be loving, and, if necessary, change."[5]

Conversation by these "rules of the game" limits the damage that comes with argument gone wrong. Argument about who worships the right One God implicitly and even usually explicitly, amounts to the colloquial, "My God is better'n your God!" Such a claim satisfies the boaster but convinces no bystanders or seekers. The boast usually relies on claims that cannot be consistently verified and that come to be seen as affirmations about faith in an authority, for example, "My Book is better'n your Book" or "My pope is better'n your rabbi or imam." Such "better'n" assertions are often related to efforts, which might be legitimate in other contexts, namely, to evangelize or proselytize. Or they can be revelatory of unpleasant and even dangerous psychological disorders. Longshoreman philosopher Eric Hoffer observed of aggressive orthodoxies within and among groups, that some creeds are born less as an expression of ardent faith than as mutual suspicion.[6] Hence, heresy-hunting, born of insecurity on the question of boundaries and adherents to the One True God, results.

We can assert "Even so, look at that!" with positive intent instead of boasting, when religious discourse or action has other purposes than worship, the theme that dominates this book. Sometimes it relates to an intellectual quest. Popular philosopher Mortimer Adler put as much energy as anyone into philosophical apologetics, believing that getting Great Ideas right would be a benefit to the human community as it faces traumatic concerns. But on numerous occasions he would confess that for decades he could prove the existence of God and talk about God, but could not find a God to worship. Then during a time of serious illness, he was converted and presented himself at the communion table in the Catholic Church. Catechists in adult Christian communities sometimes report that while instructing seekers, they will be casual or dismissive about the classic (Thomist) Catholic "proofs for the existence of God," now in popularizations of Thomas Aquinas. They say that they don't want catechumens to rely too much on such philosophical proofs. But almost always someone will come up after class and say something like, "I know you made light of these proofs, but I have to tell you, what you outlined as one of them addresses directly something with which I have been struggling." So it can be with any talk about God, which does not settle or try to settle the interfaith questions about one God, the same God, posed in this book title. Recall Jacob Neusner's discussion of such questions in the light of concern in Judaism for the *Minim*. The Abrahamic communities differ in the value they place on various motivations to deal with the "One True God" issue.

> [W]hen we survey the classical and normative sources of Judaism we produce the contradiction: Judaism declares God to be one but denies the comparable declaration of Christianity and Islam that God is uniquely one. Is the monotheism of Judaism in its classical statement different in its characteristics from the monotheism of Christianity or Islam? The answer is, only if there are variations to the

142

definition of monotheism. But while polytheism makes provision for diversity, monotheism does not. The very logic of
monotheism governs and defines the outcome: all religious
systems that affirm the unity of God necessarily speak of one
and the same God.

Developing this argument in respect to classical Judaism, Neusner
adds the comment that the community of Israel could not properly
pursue or assure justice—so central to Israel's faith—if it would be
distracted by idols. Is there room, then, in Neusner's reading of classical Judaism, for "Gentiles" to share Israel's belief in and obedience
to God? Yes, he writes, but it means that one who believes "becomes"
somehow of Israel and, in the end, is even a Jew. Accepting the Torah
is to accept God's dominion over all. Accepting Torah is how Israel
becomes Israel. The Gentile is a "different classification," but not alien-
ated from Israel, whose validity inheres in acceptance of Torah. There
is a single standard, writes Neusner for the nonidolater's identification
with Israel—the ground of being, the condition of existence.

Neusner is clear about some paradoxes and anomalies associated
with Judaism's relation to God through Torah and then with its relation to polytheists and, finally, Christians and Muslims.

> Interfaith dialogue is made possible by monotheism, which
> defines the common ground on the foundations of which
> debate can take place. Polytheism defines dialogue out of
> existence, making provision, rather, for an exchange of opin-
> ions in a spirit of tolerance. Since the polytheist religions
> lay no claim to unique possession of the truth, nothing is
> left about which to contend. That is why Judaism stands
> in judgment of Christianity and Islam specifically as these
> form explications of the meaning of the unity and unique-
> ness of God, and Judaism—so Judaism must claim—sets
> the standard for true monotheism. Christianity and Islam
> claim the same right of judgment of the competition. The
> anomaly of the classical statement of Judaism—that only

Judaism affirms authentic monotheism—yields the only true interfaith dialogue. That is defined as debate on the same issues resting on the same premises.

Bruce Chilton wrestles with the issue of sameness in ways that focus on comparison and competition. "To declare that God is the 'same' implicitly lays a claim to a superior definition of what makes for that sameness." Confronting a main theme of this book, he adds that as an analytic category in the comparative study of religion and theology, "sameness" does not appear productive. Then he adds the "but," (which parallels Levine's theme of "same" with a "yes, but . . .") when he argues that allowing the three faiths their distinctive characters without a program of discovering sameness, "does not obviate confronting their competition with each other." Note that "comparison makes that competition seem all the more acute." The faiths compete over whose God was disclosed to Abraham, and, more, "*who* that God truly is, as revealed to whom, with the demands of what kind of justice, and by the sanction of what eternal rewards and punishments." That last phrase points to another reason why this "competition" is important in the lives of believers through the centuries: getting right who God is determines eternal destinies. Chilton's climactic concluding paragraph points to the difference between claims that God is one and that God in their three traditions is the "same" remains problematic.

> Each partner can learn from the others, because they share categories of faith, even as they differ from one another in what is believed. But precisely because they all lay claim to the one God of Abraham, contradiction must attend their interactions. Each of the Abrahamic religions, while asserting that God is unique, also insists that its identification of God is uniquely true. That is why their God is one and not the same, and why believers need to acquire a taste for the fruits of difference.

That affirmation well illustrates the result of those who, puzzled by the contradictions and slighted because they are "left out" by two of the three traditions of witness and worship, still find value in the dialogue.

Vincent Cornell supplies a parable and set of distinctions that remain very useful. His story of the "Ethiopian's Dilemma," which he repeats so memorably that we do not need to retell it, prompts him to ask fellow Muslims to reflect on the theological wisdom attributed to an Ethiopian wise man. The wise man held a stick and said, "Jesus the Son of Mary does not exceed what you have said by the length of this stick," "the difference between you and me is the width of this line," which had been drawn in the sand. These are, he writes, "astute observations on the nature of the doctrinal differences between Islam and Christianity." While Cornell sees that the differences appear to be small, he does not deny the existence of the difference itself and recognizes how drastic and decisive they can be. Therefore, despite the numerous doctrinal similarities between Christianity and Islam, these have manifestly not been sufficient to bring about a truly interconfessional approach to the two religions. From a distance, the differences are thin as a stick and slight as a line in the sand. However, on closer observation these differences can be deal breakers. The most important of these, in his view, are the Christians doctrines of the Trinity and Christology. The two point to the essence of what it means to be a Christian. Yet the Qur'an denies both. Similarly, the Islamic belief in and about the Qur'an as being of Islam's essence, Christians deny, so it is also a deal breaker.

In such a reading of religious history, the little stick can be a mile wide and the width of the line in the sand might as well be as wide and deep as a canyon. Cornell's concern is to warn against ignoring creedal boundaries. As a teacher of religion in higher education he is aware that he can be perceived as a traducer who, with his definition, alters the character of religion. He quotes Oxford scholar R. C. Zaehner about academic teachers in religious studies: "The less we believe, the more we talk about what other people believe." By the way, when he turns to Muslim-Jewish relations he has the problem dealing with a smaller difference and nearer similarity. "If Jews believe in God more or less the same way as Muslims do, then what is wrong with them?" Some passages in the Qur'an lead us to ponder that question.

Cornell quotes a ninth century Muslim theologian, Abu 'Uthman al-Jahiz of Baghdad about Muslim-Jewish relations, an approach which can be applied to most interfaith issues: "Man hates the one he knows, turns against the one he sees, opposes the one he resembles, and becomes observant of the faults of those with whom he mingles; the greater the love and intimacy, the greater the hatred and estrangement."

Cornell adds: "Every act of interreligious accommodation brings up the question of boundaries," which are so important in communities. The question of this book is not whether the theologies of Islam, Christianity, and Judaism are compatible with each other, but rather whether the *God* of each religion is the *same God* as the God of the other. For Neusner, he summarizes, the "logic of monotheism" compels us to answer yes. But Cornell says the answer has to be no, when we personalize God and move from abstraction and logic. He illustrates this best by exploring the evangelical version of Protestant Christianity, which makes so much of Jesus as God in its witness to the Incarnation and the Doctrine of the Trinity. If Islam formerly was somewhat marginal to interfaith discussion when it was dominated by Jewish and Christian concerns, the new scene, in which Islam plays such a strong role, heightens concerns about worshipping the same God—or not—as such concerns are increasingly threatening and clarifying.

This book was prompted by problems raised in interfaith relations and in the interests of ordinary people, including those who study religion. At the very least, these four scholars have given us reasons not to be paralyzed even by distinctions with which they leave us when, in effect, they say once more, "Even so, look at that. . . ."

Contributor Information

Bruce D. Chilton is the Bernard Iddings Bell Professor of Religion; chaplain of the college; and executive director of the Institute of Advanced Theology at Bard College. He is a scholar of early Christianity and Judaism and is formerly Lillian Claus Professor of New Testament at Yale University. He wrote the first critical commentary on the Aramaic version of Isaiah (*The Isaiah Targum*, 1987), as well as academic studies that analyze Jesus in his Judaic context (*A Galilean Rabbi and His Bible*, 1984; *The Temple of Jesus*, 1992; *Pure Kingdom*, 1996) and explain the Bible critically (*Redeeming Time: The Wisdom of Ancient Jewish and Christian Festal Calendars*, 2002; *The Cambridge Companion to the Bible*, 2007). He founded the *Journal for the Study of the New Testament* and *The Bulletin for Biblical Research*. Active in the ministry of the Anglican Church, Dr. Chilton is rector of the Church of St. John the Evangelist in Barrytown, New York. Some of his other books include: *Rabbi Jesus: An Intimate Biography; God in Strength; Rabbi Paul: An Intellectual Biography; Judaic Approaches to the Gospels; Revelation; Trading Places; Jesus' Prayer and Jesus' Eucharist; Forging a Common Future; and Jesus' Baptism and Jesus' Healing;* and *The Way of Jesus.*

Vincent J. Cornell is Asa Griggs Candler Professor of Middle East and Islamic Studies at Emory University in Atlanta, Georgia. Since 2011 he has also been chair of the Department of Middle Eastern and South Asian Studies at Emory University. From 2000–2006, he was professor of history and director of the King Fahd Center for Middle East and Islamic Studies at the University of Arkansas. From 1991–2000, he taught at Duke University. His published works include forty articles, three books, and one book set, including *The Way of Abu Madyan* and *Realm of the Saint: Power and Authority in Moroccan Sufism.* His most recent major publication is the five-volume book set *Voices of Islam.* This comprehensive introduction to Islamic religion, thought, life, and civilization includes chapters by fifty Muslim authors, including many of the premier scholars of Islamic studies. Dr. Cornell's interests cover the entire spectrum of Islamic thought from the doctrinal and social history of Islamic mysticism to theology and political philosophy. With Bruce B. Lawrence of Duke University he is the editor of *The Wiley-Blackwell Companion to Islamic Spirituality.* He is also working on a genealogical study of the problematic of Islam and democracy. Since 2002 he has been a key participant in the annual Building Bridges seminars of Christian and Muslim scholars conducted by the Archbishop of Canterbury.

Baruch A. Levine is the Skirball Professor Emeritus of Bible and Ancient Near Eastern Studies at New York University. He has written extensively in the field of biblical and ancient Near Eastern studies. Among his publications are commentaries on *Numbers* 1–20 and *Numbers* 21–36 in *The Anchor Bible Commentary*, the commentary on *Leviticus* in *The JPS Torah Commentary* (1989), and *In the Presence of the Lord* (1974). He is past president of the Association of Jewish Studies and the Biblical Colloquium. His memberships include the Biblical Colloquium, American Oriental Society, and Society of Biblical Literature. Two volumes of his collected studies entitled *In Pursuit of Meaning*, ed. Andrew D. Gross, appeared in 2011.

Martin E. Marty is the Fairfax M. Cone Distinguished Service Professor Emeritus at the University of Chicago Divinity School, where he taught for thirty-five years and where the Martin Marty Center has since been founded to promote "public religion" endeavors. He is the author of sixty books. Marty wrote the three-volume *Modern American Religion,* and other books are *The One and the Many: America's Search for* *the Common Good; Education, Religion and the Common Good; Politics, Religion and the Common Good; Building Cultures of Trust; When Faiths Collide;* and with photographer Micah Marty, *Places Along the Way; Our Hope for Years to Come; The Promise of Winter;* and *When True Simplicity Is Gained.* He has published thirteen books in the thirteen years since retirement, including, most recently, *Dietrich Bonhoeffer's Letters and Papers from Prison: A Biography.* His *Righteous Empire: The Protestant Experience in America* won the National Book Award in 1972. He has been awarded the National Medal of the Humanities, the Medal of the American Academy of Art and Sciences, and eight honorary doctorates. He has been president of the American Society of Church History, the American Catholic Historical Association, and the American Academy of Religion.

Jacob Neusner is Distinguished Service Professor of the History and Theology of Judaism; Senior Fellow, Institute of Advanced Theology, Bard College, in Annandale-on-Hudson, New York. Born in Hartford, Connecticut, Neusner was educated at Harvard University, the Jewish Theological Seminary of America (where he received rabbinic ordination), the University of Oxford, and Columbia University. Since 1994, he has taught at Bard College. He has also taught at Columbia University, University of Wisconsin–Milwaukee, Brandeis University, Dartmouth College, Brown University, and the University of South Florida. Neusner is a member of the Institute for Advanced Study in Princeton, and a life member of Clare Hall, Cambridge University. He also served on both the National Endowment for the Humanities and the National Endowment for the Arts. Neusner has written or edited hundreds of books, including *Theology of the Oral Torah* (1998) and *Theology of the Halakhah* (2001). Awards include ten honorary degree and fourteen academic medals and prizes.

Notes

3. One God, the Same God?

1. See Chilton, "Typologies of *Memra* and the Fourth Gospel," *Targum Studies* 1 (1992): 89–100; with Paul V. M. Flesher and Bruce Chilton, *The Targums. A Critical Introduction* (Waco: Baylor University Press, 2011).

2. The preposition *pros* in Greek straightforwardly means "to" or "in relation to." This verse has in the past been rendered, "and the word was *with* God." That translation is a function of later Christian theology, in which *logos* was simply and irreducibly identified with Jesus. The prologue shows us how that identification was effectuated, without simply collating Jesus to *logos*.

3. In the Gospel, the overarching perspective is established that the *logos* is God's primordially, rather than simply Jesus' (or even Jesus' in God's). It is on that basis that Jesus can claim that the word he speaks will judge anyone who rejects him and does not accept his utterances (John 12:48-50). It is neither Jesus himself, nor what he says, that will judge such a person on the last day, but the *logos* (here functioning much as the *memra* in the Targumim). The *logos* spoken by Jesus is held to have a dynamic property, as in 15:3, where it is held to have purified those who belong to Jesus. It is Jesus, nonetheless, and no other, who is understood to speak the *logos*, and the treatment of the disciples is to reflect people's response to his word (15:20).

4. See *Legum Allegoria* I.40; *De Sacrificiis Abelis et Caini* 9; *Quod Deterius Potiori insididari soleat* 161–62; *De Migratione Abrahami* 84; *De Mutatione Nominum* 19; *De Vita Moses* 1.158; *Quod Omnis Probus Liber sit* 43.

5. Eric Francis Osborn, *Justin Martyr,* Beiträge zur hisorischen Theologie 47 (Tübingen: Mohr, 1973), 88–89.

6. See Sylvain Jean Gabriel Sanchez, *Justin Apologiste Chrétien,* Cahiers de la Revue Biblique 50 (Paris: Gabalda 2000):185–94.

7. Cf. Laura Nasrallah, "Mapping the World: Justin, Tatian, Lucian, and the Second Sophistic," *Harvard Theological Review* 98.3 (2005): 283–314.

8. Oskar Skarsaune, "Judaism and Hellenism in Justin Martyr, Elucidated From His Portrait of Socrates," in *Geschichte—Tradition—Reflexion. Festschrift für Martin Hengel zum 70. Geburtstag* III *Frühes Christentum,* ed. Hermann Lichtenberger (Tübingen: Mohr, 1996), 585–611, 599, 606.

9. See Chilton, "Typologies of Memra and the Fourth Gospel," *Targum Studies* 1 (1992): 89–100 and *Judaic Approaches to the Gospels:* International Studies in Formative Christianity and Judaism 2 (Atlanta: Scholars Press, 1994), 177–201.

10. See J. C. M. Van Winden, *An Early Christian Philosopher. Justin Martyr's Dialogue with Trypho Chapters One to Nine.* Introduction, Text, and Commentary. (Leiden: Brill, 1971), 118.

11. Philippe Bobichon, *Justin Martyr. Dialogue avec Tryphon. Édition critique*: Paradosis 47.1, 2 (Fribourg: Academic Press, 2003): 2.500.

12. See Chilton, *A Feast of Meanings. Eucharistic Theologies from Jesus through Johannine Circles:* Supplements to *Novum Testamentum* 72 (Leiden: Brill, 1994); Graham Keith, "Justin Martyr and Religious Exclusivism," *Tyndale Bulletin* 43.1 (1992): 57–80.

13. Graham N. Stanton, "Justin Martyr's *Dialogue with Trypho*: Group Boundaries, 'Proselytes' and 'God-fearers'" in *Tolerance and Intolerance in Early Judaism and Christianity,* ed. Graham N. Stanton and Guy G. Stroumsa (Cambridge: Cambridge University Press, 1998), 263–78.

14. See Chilton, "James and the (Christian) Pharisees," in *When Judaism and Christianity Began. Essays in Memory of Anthony J. Saldarini I. Christianity in the Beginning*: Supplements to the *Journal for the Study of Judaism* 85, ed. A. J. Avery-Peck, D. Harrington, J. Neusner (Leiden: Brill, 2004), 19–47.

15. Lars Hartman, *"Into the Name of the Lord Jesus": Baptism in the Early Church,* Studies of the New Testament and its World (Edinburgh: Clark, 1997), 37–50.

16. That is precisely the translation in Jacob Neusner, *The Mishnah. A New Translation* (New Haven: Yale University Press, 1988), 707. See also Pesahim 60a, cited by Hartman, *"Into the Name of the Lord Jesus,"* 49n53.

17. Hartman, *"Into the Name of the Lord Jesus,"* 47.

18. G. B. Caird, *New Testament Theology*, ed. L. D. Hurst (Oxford: Clarendon, 1994), 224.

19. For a discussion of the extension and its theological underpinnings, see Jacob Neusner and Bruce D. Chilton, *The Body of Faith: Israel and the Church* (Christianity and Judaism—The Formative Categories) (Valley Forge, PA: Trinity Press International, 1996) 129–33.

20. C. K. Barrett, *The Acts of the Apostles I: The International Critical Commentary* (Edinburgh: Clark, 1994), 108. See also Hartman, 131–33, who observes the coherence with Luke 24:44-49. That is a telling remark because it shows, together with the preaching attributed to Peter in the house of Cornelius, that the narrative of Jesus' passion was connected with the catechesis, which lead to baptism from a primitive stage.

21. Barrett, *The Acts of the Apostles I,* 129–57, presents a fine analysis on how deeply influential the text of Joel is on the speech of Peter as a whole.

22. See Bruce Chilton, *Jesus' Prayer and Jesus' Eucharist: His Personal Practice of Spirituality* (Valley Forge: Trinity Press International, 1997). Hartman, *"Into the Name of the Lord Jesus,"* 61, also approaches this idea.

23. Hartman, *"Into the Name of the Lord Jesus,"* 67–68.

24. Paul's insistence here that the rock was Christ might be intended to qualify the claims of the Petrine circle.

25. The assumption here and in Acts 2 is that Spirit makes people more articulate than they normally are. That is also the way Paul believes tongues are properly to be conceived, as opposed to those who see the gift of tongues as resulting in incoherence (see 1 Cor. 14).

26. See Hartman, *"Into the Name of the Lord Jesus,"* 133–36.

27. For a discussion, see Chilton and Jacob Neusner, *Judaism in the New Testament: Practices and Beliefs* (London: Routledge, 1995), 99–104, 108–11.

28. Hartman, *"Into the Name of the Lord Jesus,"* 140, citing Acts 8:37; 22:16.

29. Gore here is referring to the baptism in Acts 19:5-7. It would be more accurate to say that they were followers of Jesus who had formerly practiced

immersion only as taught by John (and Jesus himself, at first). But their baptism at Paul's hands brings with it the Holy Spirit.

30. He here cites Acts 4:31; 6:3, 5; 11:24.

31. Charles Gore, *The Holy Spirit and the Church* (New York: Scribner's, 1924), 112.

32. Clarke Garrett, *Spirit Possession and Popular Religion: From the Camisards to the Shakers* (Baltimore: Johns Hopkins University Press, 1987), 8.

33. Gore, *The Holy Spirit and the Church,* 113.

34. In regard to the relationship between Paul and Peter, see Jacob Neusner and Bruce D. Chilton, *Revelation: The Torah and the Bible* (Christianity and Judaism—The Formative Categories), (Valley Forge, PA: Trinity Press International, 1995), 107–28. Hartman, *"Into the Name of the Lord Jesus,"* 52, 78, 84–86, also emphasizes that, in regard to baptism, Paul should be regarded as more representative than controversial.

35. See John H. Elliott, "Peter, First Epistle of," *Anchor Bible Dictionary* 5 (New York: Doubleday, 1992), 269–78.

36. For a fuller discussion, see Jacob Neusner and Bruce Chilton. *The Intellectual Foundations of Christian and Jewish Discourse: The Philosophy of Religious Argument* (London: Routledge, 1997), 70–86.

37. The passages usually cited include Tosefta Sotah 13:21f. (which speaks of Haggai, Zechariah, and Malachi as the last of the prophets), Yoma 21b in Bavli (referring to the absence of the spirit from the Second Temple), and 1 Maccabees 4:46; 9:27 (which attests that prophecy was seen as a thing of the past). For a useful review, with ample references to the primary and secondary literature, see F. W. Horn, "Holy Spirit," *Anchor Bible Dictionary* 3 (New York: Doubleday, 1992), 260–80.

38. When John departs from the Synoptics in this manner, that is likely the result of a conscious decision. See Chilton, *Profiles of a Rabbi: Synoptic Opportunities in Reading about Jesus,* Brown Judaic Studies 177 (Atlanta: Scholars Press, 1989), 139–82.

39. See John Ashton, *Understanding the Fourth Gospel* (Oxford: Clarendon, 1991), 420–25.

40. That is why, once risen, Jesus can breath creatively on his disciples just as God breathed on the first man in Gen. 2:7; see Horn, "Holy Spirit," *Anchor Bible Dictionary* 3, 266.

41. Within the communities during the first century that heard Luke and Acts read, the irony that the movement in Antioch included an associate of the person responsible for John's execution (Luke 3:18-20; 9:7-9) and involved in Jesus' execution (Luke 23:6-12) was no doubt appreciated.

42. Because Apollos was a Hellenist, a Jew from the Greek-speaking diaspora (and Alexandria, at that; Acts 17:24), the theory that the "pneumatology" of the New Testament is a general product of Christian Hellenism is further vitiated.

43. See "John the Baptist and Jesus: History and Hypotheses," *New Testament Studies* 36 (1990): 359–74, 367–68. By way of support, the implicit criticism of Philip's practice of immersion (Acts 8:12-17) might also be mentioned. It is notable that, when Philip next baptizes (Acts 8:26-40), the Spirit plays an important role in the narrative.

44. See Horn, "Holy Spirit," *Anchor Bible Dictionary* 3, 267; he there cites additional evidence.

45. As in my translation and commentary of the Targum, departures from the Hebrew text are rendered in italics; see Chilton, *The Isaiah Targum: Introduction, Translation, Apparatus, and Notes,* The Aramaic Bible Book 11 (Wilmington: Glazier, 1987).

46. See Pierre Benoit, *Passion et résurrection du Seigneur* (Paris: Cerf, 1985), 327–53; Ashton, *Understanding the Fourth Gospel* , 382.

47. The obvious comparison is with Luke 5:4-11, where a miraculous catch of fish initiates Simon Peter's discipleship. It has frequently been suggested that Luke transposes a scene of resurrection from its original position (which John gives). In fact, any transposition is likely to have been the other way around. John delays both the apostolic forgiveness of sins (John 20:23) and baptized discipleship (John 21) until after Jesus' glorification and his breathing of the spirit on his followers.

48. It has been argued that the Gospel of Peter represents a more primitive tradition, but the fact is that the text incorporates elements from the canonical Gospels. It appears to be a pastiche, much in the vein of the longer ending of

Mark. See James H. Charlesworth and Craig A. Evans, "Jesus in the Agrapha and Apocryphal Gospels," in *Studying the Historical Jesus. Evaluations of the State of Current Research:* New Testament Tools and Studies XIX, ed. B. Chilton and C. A. Evans (Leiden: Brill, 1994), 479–533, 503–14.

49. For this reason, the consensus that John 21 did not originally belong to the Gospel is seriously to be questioned.

50. See William Graham's discussion in Jacob Neusner, Bruce Chilton, and William Graham, *Three Faiths, One God: The Formative Faith and Practice of Judaism, Christianity, and Islam* (Leiden: Brill, 2003), 240–54.

51. Ibid., 247.

52. Daniel Boyarin, *Border Lines: The Partition of Judaeo-Christianity* (Philadelphia: University of Pennsylvania, 2004).

53. Boyarin, *A Radical Jew. Paul and the Politics of Identity* (Berkeley: University of California, 1994), 85.

54. See Chilton, *Rabbi Paul. An Intellectual Biography* (New York: Doubleday, 2004).

4. The Ethiopian's Dilemma

1. Arnold Guillaume, *The Life of Muhammad: A Translation of Ibn Ishaq's Sirat Rasul Allah* (Lahore, Pakistan: Oxford University Press, 1955), 146.

2. The verses that Ja'far recited for the Negus are said to have been Qur'an 19:16–21.

3. Guillaume, *The Life of Muhammad*, 152. See also, Martin Lings, *Muhammad: His Life Based on the Earliest Sources* (London: George Allen & Unwin, 1983), 83.

4. Guillaume, *The Life of Muhammad*, 152 and Lings, *Muhammad*, 84.

5. Guillaume, *The Life of Muhammad*, 154–55.

6. This definition of Christology is based on the Anglican perspective as outlined by Alister E. McGrath in *Christian Theology: An Introduction* (Malden, Massachusetts: Wiley-Blackwell, 2011), e-book, 1156–58.

7. All translations of the Qur'an in this essay are my own from the original Arabic.

8. R. C. Zaehner, *Concordant Discord: The Interdependence of Faiths, Being the Gifford Lectures on Natural Religion Delivered at St. Andrews in 1967–1969* (Oxford: Clarendon Press, 1970), 382.

9. The term *umma* is used forty-nine times in the Qur'an. See also Qur'an 2:128: "Our Lord, make us Muslims in submission to You, and make our descendants a Muslim community in submission to You (*ummatan muslimatan laka*). Show us the places to perform our rites and turn toward us in mercy, for You are the All-Merciful, the All-Forgiving."

10. Jews are also referred to in the Qur'an by the ethnic term *al-yahud* ("the Jews") or by the phrase, *alladhina hadu*, which can roughly be translated as "those who believe in Judaism." In general, these last two appellations should be understood as referring to Jews living at the time of the Prophet Muhammad (i.e., Rabbinic Jews), whereas *Banu Isra'il* most often refers to the earlier people that English translations of the Bible call "Hebrews."

11. *The Jerusalem Bible: Reader's Edition* (New York: Doubleday, 1966), 166.

12. Scott Kugle, *Rebel Between Spirit and Law: Ahmad Zarruq, Sainthood, and Authority in Islam* (Bloomington: Indiana University Press, 2006), 89–95 and 101–8.

13. Joshua Finkel, "A Risala of al-Jahiz," *Journal of the American Oriental Society*, vol. 64 (1905), 323.

14. James W. Morris, ed. and trans., *The Master and the Disciple: an Early Islamic Spiritual Dialogue* (London and New York: I. B. Tauris and the Institute of Ismaili Studies, 2001), English text 77, Arabic text 12. "If people acted according to what is in the first book (the Torah), it would lead them toward the second (the Gospel). And if they acted in accordance with the second, that would lead them toward the third (the Qur'an), until in the end they came to act according to the latest of the books."

15. See, for example, the quotation by Justin Martyr (d. ca. 165) in Bruce Chilton's contribution to this volume: "There is to be an ultimate Law and Covenant superior to all, which now must be kept by all people who claim God's inheritance" (*Dialogue with Trypho*, 11.2–3). Although liberal Protestant and Catholic theologians have often denied supersession with respect to Judaism, this is still an open question in Christian theology.

16. Biblioteca de El Escorial, Spain (manuscript 1810, ff. 147–55v). For a more detailed discussion of this text see Vincent J. Cornell, "Islam: Theologies of Difference and Ideologies of Intolerance in Islam," in Jacob Neusner and Bruce D. Chilton eds., *Religious Tolerance in World Religions*, (West Conshohocken, PA: Templeton Foundation Press, 2008), 274–96.

17. See Hershel Shanks, "Where Mary Rested: Recovering the Kathisma," *Biblical Archaeology Review*, November-December 2006, 44–51. Shanks contends incorrectly that the Umayyads took over the Kathisma Church and turned it into a mosque.

18. According to Muslim tradition, the site where the Al Aqsa mosque was built was identified for the Caliph 'Umar by Ka'b al-Ahbar, a Jewish rabbi who converted to Islam. See Abu Bakr Muhammad ibn Ahmad al-Wasiti (d. ca. 1019), *Fada'il al-Bayt al-Muqaddas*, ed., Isaac Hasson (Jerusalem: Institute of Asian and African Studies, Hebrew University of Jerusalem, 1977), 45–46.

19. Ibid., 43–44.

20. Ibid., 82–83. Mondays and Thursdays are Torah reading days in Judaism and are the days of the supererogatory "Fast of David" in Islam.

21. See Steven M. Wasserstrom, *Religion after Religion: Gershom Scholem, Mircea Eliade, and Henry Corbin at Eranos* (Princeton: Princeton University Press, 1999).

22. On the concept of the *hanif* in pre-Islamic Arabia, see Toshihiko Izutsu, *God and Man in the Koran: Semantics of the Koranic Weltaschauung* (New York: Books for Libraries Arno Press, 1980 repr. of 1964 Keio University first edition), 112–19. Some scholars of early Islam, such as my Emory University colleague Gordon D. Newby, believe that the *hunafa'* refused to become Jews or Christians because the multiplicity of Jewish and Christian sects in Arabia made it difficult to choose which Jews or Christians to become (personal communication).

23. This poem can be found in Abu Muhammad 'Abdallah al-Ghazwani, *al-Nuqta al-azaliyya fi-l-sirr al-dhat al-Muhammadiyya* (The Eternal Point in the Mystery of the Muhammadan Essence) (Rabat: Bibliothèque Générale, manuscript 2617K). Ghazwani is one of the famous Seven Saints of the city of Marrakech, where he is known locally as *Mul al-Qusur* ("Master of the Palaces"). For further information on the life and doctrines of this impor-

tant Sufi see Vincent J. Cornell, *Realm of the Saint: Power and Authority in Moroccan Sufism* (Austin, Texas: University of Texas Press, 1998), 219–29 and 240–64.

24. Farid al-Din al-'Attar, *The* Ilahi-Nama *or Book of God of Farid al-Din 'Attar*, trans. John Andrew Boyle (Manchester, U.K.: Manchester University Press, 1976), 28. The creative command "Be!" refers to (Qur'an 2:117).

25. Ibid., 29.

26. In the book *al-Insan al-Kamil* (The Perfect Human Being), the Iraqi Sufi 'Abd al-Karim al-Jili (d. 1428) states: "Each religious sect worships God as God desires to be worshipped, for He created them for Himself, not for themselves. Thus, they exist just as they were fashioned. [God] may He be glorified and exalted, manifests His names and attributes to these sects by means of His essence and all of the sects worship Him [in their own way]." See 'Abd al-Karim al-Jili, *al-Insan al-kamil fi ma'rifat al-awakhir wa al-awa'il* vol. 2 (Cairo, 1981), 122.

27. Kaufmann Kohler, *Jewish Theology: Systematically and Historically Considered* (New York: MacMillan e-book edition of the 1918 original), 70.

28. Ibid., 71.

29. Ibid., 71–72 and *The Jewish Virtual Library*, "Articles of Faith," http://www.jewishvirtuallibrary.org/jsource/Judaism/articles_of_faith.html

30. Kohler, *Jewish Theology*, 79

31. Ibid., 116–17.

32. Semantically, the term *insan* for "human being" in Arabic is nongendered and has long been understood as such by Muslim commentators of the Qur'an. The use of the masculine pronoun for generic purposes in verses such as this is merely a linguistic convention.

33. Kohler, *Jewish Theology*, 228.

34. Quoted in ibid., 224–25.

35. See Michael Marlowe, "The Only Begotten Son," http://www.bible-researcher.com/only-begotten.html.

36. Millard J. Erickson, *Christian Theology*, 2nd ed. (Grand Rapids, Mich.: Baker Academic e-book edition, 2011), 1855.

37. The website ChristianBooks.com describes Erickson's doctrinal stance as follows: "Erickson writes from a conservative, evangelical, Baptist perspective.

He is reformed, but not ardently Calvinistic." (http://www.christianbook
.com/christian-theology-second-edition-millard-erickson/9780801021824/
pd/21820)

38. Ibid., 1905–06. Erickson's *Christian Theology* is commonly regarded as the
standard textbook for conservative evangelical systematic theology. Thus, his
interpretation of Christology can be regarded as broadly representative of
this highly influential movement in American Christianity.

39. McGrath, *Christian Theology*, 1148. Alister McGrath is an Anglican theo-
logian who is currently professor of Theology, Ministry, and Education at
Kings College London and head of the Centre for Theology, Religion and
Culture at the University of London.

40. See Geoffrey Wainwright, *Doxology: The Praise of God in Worship, Doctrine,
and Life* (Oxford, U.K.: Oxford University Press, 1984).

41. See James B. Torrance, *Worship, Community, and the Triune God of Grace*
(Downer's Grove, Ill.: InterVarsity Press, 1997).

42. McGrath, *Christian Theology*, 1147–48.

43. I had the pleasure of sitting next to Bishop Cragg when he made this comment on January 18, 2002.

44. Miroslav Volf, *Allah: A Christian Response* (New York: Harper Collins, 2011).
This work is written primarily from a Roman Catholic perspective. In my
opinion Volf's arguments are weakened by an overly magisterial approach
to Christian and Islamic orthodoxy and serious misinterpretations of the
Qur'an. For example he writes, "The Qur'an suggests that Christians 'join
gods' to God by considering Jesus Christ and the Holy Spirit to be divine
(see Al Baqarah, 2:135)." (E-book edition, 226) Although this verse of the
Qur'an states that Abraham "did not join gods with God," there is no mention in it of combining Christ and the Holy Spirit. Rather, as I have dem-
onstrated above, the theological problem with Christianity from a Qur'anic
point of view is more about combining the Son and the Father.

45. See David Marshall, Campion Hall Seminar Papers, "Christian Theological
Engagement with Islam," Berkeley Center for Religion, Peace, and World
Affairs, Georgetown University, Washington D.C., July 26, 2012, (http://
berkleycenter.georgetown.edu/publications/campion-hall-seminars-papers
-on-christian-theological-engagement-with-islam).

46. Volf preselects the theologies to be compared under the pretext of normativity: "Now that I have identified which Muslims and Christians we are talking about (those who embrace the normative traditions of their respective religions) and what we are looking for (sufficient similarity in beliefs about God), the examination can start" (Volf, *Allah*, 279).

47. Ibid., 366.

48. Ibid., 367.

49. Tomoko Masuzawa, *The Invention of World Religions or How European Universalism Was Preserved in the Language of Pluralism* (Chicago: The University of Chicago Press, 2005), 75n7.

50. Edward W. Said, *Culture and Imperialism* (New York: Vintage Books, 1994), 32.

51. Ibid., 33.

Epilogue: But Even So, Look at That!

1. See Edward Rothstein, Herbert Muschamp, and Martin E. Marty, *Visions of Utopia* (New York: Oxford, 2003), 49–51

2. Alasdair MacIntyre, "The Virtues, the Unity of a Human Life and the Concept of a Tradition," in *Why Narrative? Readings in Narrative Theology*, ed. Stanley Hauerwas and L. Gregory Jones (Grand Rapids, Mich.: Eerdrmans, 1989), 101–02.

3. George Santayana, *Reason in Religion* in *The Life of Reason*. 5 vol. (Toronto: University of Toronto Libraries, 2011. *The Life of Reason* originally published in 1906.), 236.

4. Georg Simmel, "The Stranger," in *The Sociology of Georg Simmel*, trans. Kurt Wolff (New York: Free Press, 1950), f02, 406.

5. David Tracy, *Plurality and Ambiguity* (San Francisco: Harper & Row, 1987), 18–19.

6. Eric Hoffer, *The True Believer* (San Francisco: Harper & Row, 1959), 114–15.